Kids Who Have Too Much

Kids Who Have Too Much

Dr. Ralph E. Minear

AND

William Proctor

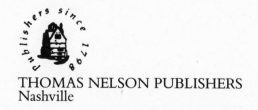

THOMAS NELSON PUBLISHERS
Nashville

Published in Nashville, Tennessee, by Thomas Nelson, Inc. and distributed in Canada by Lawson Falle, Ltd., Cambridge, Ontario.

Printed in the United States of America.

Scripture quotations are from THE NEW KING JAMES VERSION of the Bible. Copyright © 1979, 1980, 1982, Thomas Nelson, Inc., Publishers.

ISBN 0-8407-4251-7

1 2 3 4 5 6 — 92 91 90 89

Contents

Kids Who Have Too Much

Chapter One

The Dangers of Having Too Much

Not long ago, a mother brought Dana, a little girl who was just about to turn five years old, into my office for her regular checkup. Since I was aware that Dana wasn't even in kindergarten yet, I tried to describe what I was doing in the clearest, simplest terms I could muster.

When I began to refer to the "muscle on the front of the arm" that had been hurting her, however, her mother stopped me. "Oh, you can just say 'bicep,'" the mother said. "She knows all those anatomical terms. Don't you, Dana?"

Actually, as it turned out, Dana *didn't* know the terms. Her mother had been drilling her, but the girl hadn't been interested enough to learn all the technical language that was being thrown at her. Still, the mother wouldn't give up, even as I was conducting the exam. When Dana would hesitate over a term like *palate* as I was examining her mouth, or *iris* as I was looking into her eyes, the mother pressed her until she got the name and pronunciation just right.

This constant pressure to learn, even in the midst of a stressful medical examination, finally caused the youngster to collapse into tears—and I suspect she didn't leave the doctor's office that day with a very happy memory. On later meetings with this mother and child, I learned that Dana was having what seemed to be stress-related problems, such as a frequently upset stomach and periodic headaches, so I suggested that the mother not try to turn her daughter into an adult before she had matured a little more.

"There's plenty of time for her to learn big words and take in adult information," I said. "In fact, if you just let her learn at her own pace, I'm sure she'll move ahead at a rapid rate. You can make the information and opportunities for learning available at home, but don't push it. After all, she's still a child, and she has to develop at a child's rhythm. If you can just teach her to love learning—at the same time that you let her know you love her—you'll find that she'll move ahead quickly."

Unfortunately, this mother kept pushing Dana, and eventually, the girl developed problems with bed-wetting. When the emotional and physical reactions got serious enough, the mother finally got the message—she was pressing too hard to give her child too much information in too short a period of time.

Dana was a victim of a new disease that I've begun to diagnose in my pediatric practice. I call this malady the "Rich Kids Syndrome," because the children *have too much of something*—whether it's pressure to perform, freedom, money, food, protection, or parental sacrifice. This disease is almost as common in middle-class families and even in poor families as in those with a great deal of wealth.

The children who are afflicted by this syndrome may suffer from many of the same problems that beset affluent, high-achieving adults. For example, bodies and minds may show such symptoms as the following:

- ▶ periodic nausea
- ▶ headaches
- ▶ eating disorders
- ▶ high anxiety
- ▶ depression
- ▶ a variety of phobias
- ▶ hypertension

A plethora of other physical and mental problems may also occur.

However, there are often distinctive age-related expressions of the underlying emotional and physical wounds. Specific youthful difficulties may include bed-wetting, maladjustment at school, an inability to relate productively to peers or adults, and a variety of other such social and personal problems.

Think about your own family situation for a moment. Ask yourself a few key questions about how you deal with your child.

▶ Do you frequently buy him presents, even though it's not his birthday or some other special occasion?

▶ Do you have to postpone or eliminate other family events or expenditures because you have to pay for private school or a summer camp?

▶ Do you allow him to watch more than a half-hour of television a day?

▶ Do you take her on "cultural excursions," such as to museums or concerts, when she really doesn't want to go and perhaps causes a scene after she gets there?

▶ Does the gift your child wants for each special occasion have to be bigger or cost more than the last gift?

▶ Do you feel you and your child are getting overloaded with activities such as music lessons, Little League, church choir, Hebrew classes, karate class, or scouting?

▶ Does your son or daughter regularly say, "But, Mom [Dad], I want to stay at home and play this afternoon"?

▶ Does your youngster have trouble concentrating on schoolwork or other activities?

▶ Does your child expect a financial or material reward for every favor or good deed performed?

▶ Does it frequently seem that your child is asking for money or material goods to the virtual exclusion of pursuing family relationships?

▶ Does your child select friends for their material worth?

▶ On balance, does your son or daughter seem too selfish and self-centered?

▶ Does your child often say, "I've nothing to do" or "Why do we have to do that—I've already been to that museum?"

If your answer to any of these questions is yes, you may be the parent of a "kid who has too much"; and the implications of this phenomenon are what this book is all about.

Of course, in themselves, these material things or other seeming advantages that children have aren't bad or undesirable. On the contrary, rightly used, they can get a youngster off to a fast, effective start in realizing his full potential in life. But sometimes, it's possible to get too much of a good thing, to get good things in the wrong way, or to receive "advantages" with the wrong messages attached. When that happens, the Rich Kids Syndrome may arise, often with seriously negative or even tragic results.

What are some of the signs that this syndrome is afoot in our society and perhaps even in your family? Consider a few concrete manifestations that other doctors and I have encountered in pediatric practice in Boston and other locations around the country.

The "Perfect" Child

Myrna, a highly accomplished businesswoman, became pregnant and announced, only partly in jest, "This child had better be perfect because it's going to cost me $10,000 out-of-pocket immediately!"

When asked about the specific amount, she replied, "That's the amount of money I'm going to have to give up. With a kid, I won't be able to accept an out-of-town job that I've been offered that would give me a $10,000 raise."

She went on to recount in a jocular tone all the other expenses she expected to incur in the ensuing months and years because of the child's presence: money for private schools, camps, college. The list seemed endless!

Her husband, Sam, joined in the "joke," too. For him, the child was almost a status symbol. He was quite proud the youngster was going to "cost so much" and, by natural inference, grow up to be thoroughly accomplished, a worthy product of his high-achieving parents who could afford to pay for the best.

"This child had just *better* be perfect!" Sam repeated, echoing Myrna's sentiments with a smile. Only it wasn't a happy smile. A grimness in his and his wife's expressions said far more than the good humor they were trying to project.

After their son was born, it became evident just how high their expectations for the boy were—and how far they were destined to fall. The child was born with a "lazy eye," one that didn't move normally and had a tendency to be crossed. This turn of events upset both Sam and Myrna immensely. After all, how could adults of their talents and credentials produce a youngster who wasn't perfect?

Then, Myrna tried to breast-feed the baby, but she was unsuccessful because of a lack of milk and also because the child wasn't able to suck properly. Consequently, the boy began to lose weight, and after trying various feeding techniques, he finally had to be placed on a bottle with formula.

Myrna kept up a brave front for months, trying as hard as she could to correct the problems or to ignore them, always hoping they would miraculously go away. Also, to compensate for what she perceived as the youngster's deficiencies, she placed him in a variety of superbaby programs at a young age. There were foreign language courses, "baby math," swimming, and so many other activities that by the time he was three, the boy had no free time at all.

Finally, the youngster started showing signs of hyperactivity. He had been programmed to go frantically in too many different directions at a young age. The pressures, combined with a natural tendency toward hyperactivity, triggered a major set of emotional problems.

At this point, Myrna's public face collapsed in a wave of tears. "I must tell you that the 'perfect mother' has failed," she told her pediatrician.

"What are you talking about?" he asked.

"I've blown it completely with this boy," she replied. "I couldn't breast-feed properly. I tried to correct that physical problem with his eye by giving him a head start intellectually and athletically, but he's not really responding. And now, hyperactivity. I've failed!"

The doctor spent a great deal of time explaining to Myrna why it was absolutely wrong for her to equate any of these problems in her child with her failure to be "perfect." "Nobody expects you to be perfect," he said. "Nobody, that is, except maybe yourself! You *can't* be perfect, so just relax. Back off and stop trying to push all these programs on your son. Set aside some time just to be with him and love him. Change your expectations. Children don't always turn out the way the parent expects."

Gradually, by changing the behavior within the family, Myrna and Sam were able to take some of the pressure off their son, and before long, things seemed to be improving. But these parents will have to continue to pay careful attention to giving their child more room just to be himself. They mustn't attempt to turn him into a clone of themselves or force him to meet all their expectations.

The Consequences of Culture-Cramming

Another well-educated young couple decided that they were going to give their four-year-old daughter a maximum amount of exposure to the cultural outlets in their city.

"After all, what's the point in living near museums, theaters, and such if you don't make full use of them?" the father asked rhetorically, obviously assuming that the answer to his question was, "There's *no* point!"

Ironically, as it turned out, a problem developed that centered on these very outings. Or to be more precise, it was the *way* the parents conducted the outings.

In the first place, the mother and the father did not adequately consider the reality that they were adults and their child was a preschooler. They had read somewhere that you should "never talk baby talk to a child—always talk adult to adult." So they took this advice to an extreme and treated their daughter, Heather, like a little adult. They required her to spend the same amount of time in museums as they did. They took her to sophisticated, often quite lengthy plays. And they literally *dragged* her to three-hour concerts at the local symphony hall.

The main idea behind all this "culture-cramming," as I called it, wasn't so bad. To be sure, with the right kind of exposure, a small child can begin to get a good foundation in appreciating the theater, the arts, and music. But obviously, the approach that this family took wasn't suited to the needs or interests of the child. As a result, the little girl, who frequently became bored and tired with all the adult cultural events, began to resist and "act up." That is, she began to behave in ways that were inappropriate to the situations in which her parents had placed her.

For example, Heather would start to whine, talk loudly, and otherwise act disruptively in the middle of a violin solo. Or she would start to cry and argue at just the moment when the actor on the stage was trying to evoke a critical mood in the audience or get a key message across about the plot. The parents were frequently embarrassed as other spectators said "shh" or asked them directly to keep Heather quiet.

In this case, I don't blame the other adults who were getting annoyed. After all, they had come to the cultural events to enjoy themselves, not to observe young parents trying to control or discipline their child!

Nor do I blame Heather. She had been overloaded with cultural events and adult stimulation. She was a "kid who had too much" adult culture. Before long, she let her parents know about her dissatisfaction in the only way she knew—by complaining loudly or throwing a fit.

Fortunately, Heather didn't suffer any perceptible emotional damage as a result of her parents' unwise cultural aspirations for her. She made enough nuisance of herself soon enough that they quickly adjusted their expectations for her.

What's the situation in this family now? I'm sorry to say that they still haven't quite learned how to get cultural influences across to her in a way that's right for her age and emotional development. But at least they're refraining from putting the excessive pressure on her that was causing so many problems.

Another set of parents has done a better job introducing culture into the life of their child. They take their son to museums, but they try to pick *only* exhibits and events that they expect to interest him.

For example, if they hear of a workshop for children that is being held in conjunction with an art or a historical exhibit, they'll make plans to attend. That way, the boy will have an opportunity for play and fun as well as for an educational experience. Also, they don't take the boy to most adult plays, though they have frequently attended the children's theater in their community. When their son gets a little older, they plan to take him to more sophisticated offerings, but not before then.

In addition to choosing child-oriented cultural programs, this couple tries to *prepare* their youngster for events beforehand. On one occasion, they got tickets to a play based on Shays' Rebellion, which occurred just after the American Revolution. The point of the play, which was designed for viewing by older children, was to show how the rebellion had influenced the calling of the Constitutional Convention.

Because their son, who was only eight years old, hadn't taken American history at school, the parents decided to make things more interesting for him by supplementing his lack of background information. They bought a book at the youngster's reading level that told the story of the early American republic, including Shays' Rebellion. Throughout, the narrative was written in lively and under-standable terms for elementary school children. By the time the family entered the theater for the one-hour production, the boy had been thoroughly prepped. Not only that, he was eagerly looking forward to seeing a dramatic presentation of the historical events that he had just read about.

Yes, every child should be exposed to culture, but there's never any justification for a cram course or overexposure, which often will even cause many adults to become "overdosed." Rather, it's impor-tant to be sure your child has just enough culture in the amounts that he personally can handle.

The Public School Solution

One family, who really couldn't afford it, decided to send both children to private school. "We just feel that the public schools in this area don't offer enough, and we want our children to have the best, even if means sacrificing ourselves," the father said.

Their eleven-year-old daughter did quite well in private school. As the parents noted, she really "blossomed" in her classes and made great strides forward with the individual attention she received in her reading and other courses. But the nine-year-old son was a dif-ferent story. The boy, Larry, began to do so poorly that his teacher called his mother and said, "I'm sorry to report this, but Larry is actually failing fourth grade this year."

"How can any smart child, in a private school that's costing an arm and a leg, fail fourth grade?" the father stormed when his wife broke the news to him that evening.

But when the couple met with the teacher and principal, they learned that there were indeed some solid reasons why Larry was having trouble. It seemed that the boy wasn't completing his class-work assignments, and in general, he appeared to be totally unable to keep up with the other children.

Also, he was having difficulties with social adjustments. He fre-quently played by himself, had few friends, and seemed to have trou-ble fitting in with children who had many more possessions—such as high-priced clothes, toys, and sports equipment—than he did. In addition, he frequently disrupted the class by asking to go to the bathroom.

"He's always making trouble for his teacher and the other children," the principal told the parents.

At the suggestion of the teacher, the parents brought the boy in to see me, just to determine whether or not there was some organic problem. To begin with, I scheduled a number of tests. For example, after hearing that he was going to the bathroom so often, I wanted to be sure that he didn't have diabetes. So I checked that out but came up with a negative result.

After conducting a thorough examination, I found nothing physically wrong with the boy. Furthermore, as I looked over his intelligence test scores, I got a picture of a child who was scoring at the very top of his age group. At the same time, however, psychological tests revealed a boy who was extremely anxious and in many respects unsure of himself—as might be expected, given his experiences at school. Despite these difficulties, though, there seemed to be no serious mental problems.

"I have to conclude from all this that your child doesn't belong in that school," I finally told his parents. "From what you and he have told me, I don't think he's receiving the kind of sensitive attention at school that he needs at this point in his life. A good counselor might be able to provide that. But this private school, though it has other things to offer, doesn't have a permanent psychological counselor on staff."

The parents began to look around at other options and decided to put the boy in a local public school, which had a team of counselors who seemed attuned to children with his problems.

Sure enough, after only three or four months in the new school environment, Larry settled down and began to operate at his true potential. Among other things, he stopped going to the bathroom so often. Also, he developed a set of friends with whom he frequently made dates to play after school.

The public school didn't have the small classes or some of the other one-to-one benefits of the private school, but those expensive educational accouterments weren't what Larry needed. He was a child who had been given too much of the wrong kind of education. When his parents realized this fact, they provided the real attention that he required—at considerably less cost to the family.

These are just a few vignettes to illustrate how a child can have too much of a variety of things and end up facing a morass of emotional and physical difficulties. Perhaps you identify with some of these situations as you compare them with your own family. After all, most of us want to do all that we possibly can for our children. We want to give them every conceivable advantage and place them in a position to make the best of their natural abilities and interests when they reach adulthood.

But still, it's possible to go too far. And if we do go too far with our youngsters, serious trouble may be in store for them and the rest of the family. Many cultural danger signals have come to my attention in recent years, both in my own pediatric practice and in reports in the national news media.

For example, one year in private school, even for those in kindergarten, can cost $7,000 or more in some parts of the country. The cost may be $10,000 or more for the higher grades and boarding schools. Families who choose this educational route for their children are often asking for unbearable financial pressures, which may eventually be communicated to their children.

A gold-plated crib goes for $2,400. Does a child really sleep any better in such a bed?

A satin-and-lace baby comforter sells for $120. What's wrong with a plain cotton or wool blanket or perhaps a free quilt made by a parent or grandparent?

For $21, an infant can get a forty-five minute "workout" and an "infant massage." Obviously not a service performed by loving parental hands!

A giant-sized toy panda was recently on sale at F.A.O. Schwarz, the big New York City toy store, for $220. And of course that's a relatively cheap item. The cost of intricate mechanical toys can easily run into thousands of dollars.

Eight weeks' worth of fancy summer camp for a child of any age can easily go for $3,000 to $4,000. Many parents fail to take advantage of much more economical—and equally fun and educational—day camps in their areas.

A young boy's cologne sells for $15.50 per .85 fluid ounce bottle. The parents may like it, but what about the boy?

Designer party dresses may cost $100 or more for a preschooler, and the cost mounts considerably as the girl's age increases. Yet what do such purchases communicate to the child about the value of money?

Some of these expenses obviously stretch the resources of many families to the limit—and perhaps beyond. Others creep up by $10, $50, and $100 increments until, before parents know it, a huge part of the family budget is going into possessions, services, and "advantages" for the youngsters that will quickly be discarded or outgrown. Also, there are many nonmonetary items with which we overwhelm our children: culture, information, education, you name it. We provide, push, and force-feed our youngsters with these influences, often without asking the simple question, "Have they had enough?"

Many times, the result of all this splurging and attention is not at all happy. In fact, it may be devastating. Reflect for a moment on the tragedy of Jennifer Levin, the prep school graduate who was killed in Central Park in 1986. Her companion for the evening, Robert Chambers, also a former New York City prep school student, was charged with her death.

These children of privilege had been drinking on the night of the death at a fashionable Upper East Side bar. Jennifer and Robert knew many of the "right" people; they lived at fashionable addresses; and they frequented many high-society parties. They seemed to "have it all," including plenty of free time and large amounts of money to spend. Yet in this case, as well as in others less dramatic, the final curtain came down on a scene of tragedy. (We'll talk more about why this happened in chapter 3.)

These may be extreme cases of the Rich Kids Syndrome, involving "kids who have too much." But such examples should still serve as a warning to all of us who sometimes feel we are willing to go to any length to provide our children with the very best.

In the following pages, I deal mostly with more ordinary, garden-variety cases of this phenomenon. As we proceed, I will encourage you to take a closer look at your family and your children. Among other things, you'll be asked to consider whether you may be giving your children.

- ▶ too much freedom, which can result in a lack of discipline and moral guidance;
- ▶ too many material goods as a substitute for the time you should be spending with them;
- ▶ too much pressure to perform, with resulting stress that may cause your children to cave in and *under*achieve;

▶ too much information and too little instruction about how to *use* that information maturely;

▶ too much protection, with too little preparation for the difficult challenges of the real world;

▶ too much independence, accompanied by too little practical advice about how to deal with the pains of growing up;

▶ too much food and far too little advice about good nutrition; and

▶ too much parental sacrifice, with too little education at home about the basic responsibilities of life.

But stating the problem is only the first step. My *main* purpose throughout this book is to provide you with the necessary tools to enable you, your family, and your children to break free of the Rich Kids Syndrome. Then, you'll be in a position to begin to use your possessions and advantages in a wiser and more productive way.

First of all, to see just how deeply enmeshed you are in the syndrome, you'll be asked to respond to some questions I frequently pose to the parents of my patients. This "Test for the Rich Kids Syndrome" will help you pinpoint your level of risk as well as the risk level of your children.

Also, we'll spend some time later considering ways that you can learn and teach greater moderation in managing your material possessions; develop a stronger family value system; help your children overcome bad or dangerous habits, such as those related to drugs and sex; and show your youngsters how to cope with the distinctive stresses that plague contemporary young people.

Now, let's determine the extent to which you and your children may be caught in the clutches of the Rich Kids Syndrome.

Chapter Two

Is Your Child a Victim of the Rich Kids Syndrome?

To help you determine if the Rich Kids Syndrome is a threat to your family, I've prepared the following test. Your responses will assist you in ascertaining whether or not your child is a victim or potential victim of the syndrome. Then, with a clearer idea of where you stand, you'll be in a better position to take appropriate steps to correct any problems.

The Test for the Rich Kids Syndrome

Answer each question with a "true" or "yes," or a "false" or "no." Then, at the end of the test, I'll provide some guidelines for you to evaluate the level of risk for your family and your child. *Note:* The male and female pronouns have been used interchangeably to indicate that each question applies both to boys and to girls.

_____ **1.** My child watches more than a half-hour of television each day.

_____ **2.** My child watches more than an hour of television each day.

_____ **3.** My child watches more than two hours of television each day.

_____ **4.** My child often seems unenthusiastic, bored, or complacent when he receives a gift.

_____ **5.** One or both parents in our family relieve tension by shopping.

_____ **6.** Conflicts, anxieties, or depressions in our family are frequently settled with a checkbook. (For example, the husband may resort to buying something for the wife if he has offended her. Or one or both spouses may insist on a vacation as "necessary relief" or an "escape valve" from pressure, regardless of the cost or the money available.)

_____ **7.** My child doesn't seem to know where the limits are in terms of purchasing things.

_____ **8.** My child is frequently tired.

_____ **9.** My child has more headaches, stomachaches, nausea, or other physical problems than seem normal for someone his age.

_____ **10.** My child often "acts up" in public by throwing temper tantrums, arguing loudly, or otherwise behaving inappropriately.

_____ **11.** Sometimes, my child will take candy or other merchandise from a store shelf, even though no one has bought it for her or given her permission to take it.

_____ **12.** My child is very well provided for, but I personally often feel strapped for cash.

_____ **13.** I occasionally feel resentful because I have to sacrifice so much to give my child what he wants.

_____ **14.** I think I've identified some important talents in my child, but I can't seem to get her to take advantage of them.

_____ **15.** My child has many more toys or clothes than he regularly uses.

_____ **16.** Frequently, I'll buy something for my youngster, and then she'll discard it after playing with it only a few times.

_____ **17.** My child is very reluctant to give away any old toys, clothes, or other possessions.

_____ **18.** At least 10 percent of the family's net income (after taxes) is spent on "extras" for my child.
Note: "Extras" would include such items as private schooling, camps, and toys; the figure would exclude "basics" such as the child's food, allotments for housing, or expenses for necessary clothing.

_____ **19.** At least 20 percent of the family's net income (after taxes) is spent on "extras" for my child. (The "Note" in #18 also applies here.)

_____ **20.** My child engages in at least two important activities a week (requiring a minimum of three hours a week) in addition to school.
Note: These activities may include such things as going to the library to read or check out books for home reading, music lessons and practice, organized sports, dance classes and practice, study of a second language, children's choir, or crafts instruction.

_____ **21.** My child engages in at least three important activities a week (requiring a minimum of four hours a week) in addition to school. (The "Note" in #20 also applies here.)

_____ **22.** I take my child to at least one cultural event a week (museums, concerts, expositions, lectures, exhibitions).

_____ **23.** I take my child to at least two cultural events a week.

_____ **24.** My child spends at least four waking hours a week with baby sitters or other caretakers or services.

_____ **25.** My child spends at least eight waking hours a week with baby sitters or other day-care-type people or services.

_____ **26.** My child spends at least twelve waking hours a week with baby sitters or other caretakers or services.

_____ **27.** My child spends at least twenty waking hours a week with baby sitters or other caretakers or services.

_____ **28.** I try to be very sure that my child avoids situations that might result in even mild physical injury.

_____ **29.** My child is a sensitive, artistic type who generally needs to be protected or separated from boisterous or rough youngsters.

_____ **30.** I try to give my child every possible advantage, even when it means my spouse and I must make significant sacrifices.

_____ **31.** I'm trying to get my child to change his interests toward things that I know will be important to him later in life.

_____ **32.** My child spends most of her time hanging out with friends and very little time at school-sponsored activities, such as sports or clubs.

_____ **33.** My child is overweight.

_____ **34.** My youngster eats far too much junk food, but I don't seem to be able to do anything about it.

_____ **35.** My child pretty much determines where we go on vacations.

_____ **36.** I think my child may have a problem with drugs, including alcohol.

_____ **37.** I have reason to believe my youngster is having some trouble with sex.

_____ **38.** I have private conversations with my child less than once a week.

_____ **39.** I rarely or never discipline or punish my child.

_____ **40.** I give my youngster money whenever he asks for it.

_____ **41.** I give my child an allowance without requiring her to work for any part of it.

_____ **42.** I have a child, ten years old or younger, who receives an allowance of at least $5 a week without having to do any work or household chores for it.

_____ **43.** I have a child, eleven years old or older, who receives an allowance of at least $10 a week without having to do any work or household chores for it.

_____ **44.** My child receives an allowance of at least $20 a week without having to work or do chores for any part of it.

_____ **45.** My youngster complains frequently that he is under too much pressure to perform at school or in some other activity.

_____ **46.** My child has been shielded from the influence of any special religious faith.

_____ **47.** I usually try to avoid telling my youngster that a particular moral code is right or wrong. I just leave most decisions about right and wrong up to her.

_____ **48.** No one else is usually around when my child comes home from school.

_____ **49.** My child makes up his own mind about when he wants to get home at night after a date or an outing with friends.

_____ **50.** My child has a problem with bed-wetting.

_____ **51.** My child clings to me or my spouse when strangers are around.

_____ **52.** My youngster has considerable difficulty making new friends.

_____ **53.** My child seems unable to play with other children amicably unless he gets his own way.

_____ **54.** I spend five or more hours a week in private conversations with my child.

_____ **55.** My child often seems depressed or "down" about life.

_____ **56.** My child wakes up as a result of nightmares several times a week.

_____ **57.** My youngster seems to be plagued by an unusual number of fears.

_____ **58.** I think my child may suffer from a serious eating disorder, such as anorexia nervosa or bulimia.

_____ **59.** My child often has symptoms of nervousness, such as bouts of nausea before new or challenging experiences.

_____ **60.** My child breaks into tears fairly often for no apparent reason.

_____ **61.** My child is alone in the house by himself at least one hour per week.

_____ **62.** My child is alone in the house by herself at least four hours per week.

_____ **63.** My child will never do a chore at home without receiving an expensive gift as a reward.

_____ **64.** Many of the values in our household have a financial bottom line.

_____ **65.** The most important goal for my child is that she be better off financially than I am.

_____ **66.** I feel guilty if my child isn't dressed like his classmates or if he doesn't have the same possessions as his friends.

_____ **67.** I rarely have one meal a day with my child.

_____ **68.** The weekend is the only time I have with my child.

_____ **69.** The main time I spend with my child is when we go to movies, go shopping, eat out, or watch TV.

_____ **70.** My child controls what and when she eats.

_____ **71.** My child gets almost every gadget or material item that her friends have.

_____ **72.** My child is almost always first in the neighborhood to have the most expensive toy or the latest gadget.

_____ **73.** I don't know what my child knows about sex.

_____ **74.** I don't know what my child values most in her life.

_____ **75.** I want my child to be on his own by the time he's eighteen.

_____ **76.** My child is spoiled, and I don't know how to "unspoil" him.

_____ **77.** My child respects only those people who appear to be wealthy or live a "rich" life.

_____ **78.** Absolutely nothing impresses my youngster.

_____ **79.** As a parent, I have practically every hour of the day planned so that my child rarely has any free or "down" time.

_____ **80.** As a parent, I spend much time rehearsing what my young child should do in potentially dangerous situations—e.g., when approached by a stranger, when lost in a crowd, when accompanying friends and their parents on an outing, when with a new baby sitter.

_____ **81.** I have never examined in depth the roles that money and materialism occupy in my family.

_____ **82.** It's foolish to limit resources that I might spend on my child because she will be with me only a short time.

_____ **83.** My child will select his own values about material goods, irrespective of what I teach or suggest.

_____ **84.** I don't know my child's spiritual or religious beliefs.

_____ **85.** My child doesn't often discuss her joys, fears, beliefs, mistakes, and hopes with me.

_____ **86.** The family never takes a vacation together.

_____ **87.** The family never has a "family conference" so that family members can raise questions and air their concerns.

_____ **88.** My child always spends her vacations away from home.

_____ **89.** I wish I had more money for myself or general family needs instead of having to spend so much on my child.

How to Evaluate Your Answers

Here's how to score your family and determine the risk for your child. First, count all the "true" or "yes" answers. Next, determine which category you're in.

▶ *Low risk:* 10 or fewer "yes" answers.
▶ *Medium risk:* 11 to 22 "yes" answers.

▶ *High risk:* 23 to 45 "yes" answers.
▶ *Critical risk:* 46 to 66 "yes" answers.
▶ *Immediate professional attention probably required* (from medical, psychological, or religious counselors): 67 or more "yes" answers.

Caution: If you answered "true" or "yes" to these questions—8, 9, 10, 11, 33, 36, 37, 50, 55, 57, 58, 59, and 60—you should seek professional help regardless of your total score.

If you scored in the low-risk category, you and your child probably don't have to worry about being in any danger from the Rich Kids Syndrome. The only exception would be if you know your child is in trouble with drugs, sex, or some other emotional or physical problem that involves immediate danger.

If you scored in the medium-risk category, you may be in no current danger. But you should still consider taking steps to adjust the situation in your family so that your child can benefit from firmer values, more responsible independence, and a better management of material possessions and opportunities. The following chapters of this book should help you to develop an effective personal strategy.

If you reached the high-risk level, it's imperative that you act immediately to correct the situation. In many cases, concerned and informed parents can formulate the necessary strategies and take the required steps to set things on a more productive path.

In the event that you scored above 45 "yes" answers—at the criticial-risk level—your family and your child may already need some serious medical, psychological, or spiritual assistance.

Finally, if you ended up in the 67 or above category, seek professional help immediately!

What Else Do You Need to Know about This Test?

The questions in this test are based on observations from my own clinical practice, on studies of the medical and psychological literature, and on relevant social and cultural trends noted by experts in several nonmedical fields. As we move through the different sections of this book, I'll refer to much of this source material, and that should give you more reason to say, "*Now* I see why he asked this or that question!"

For now, let me just mention briefly five basic considerations that underlie many of the questions in the test and also frequently play a major role in the rise of the Rich Kids Syndrome. These might be called the five "affluenza factors" because they reflect both the causes and the symptoms of a social pattern—rooted in affluence or the aspiration to affluence—that has gripped parents and families in our society.

Affluenza Factor #1: Children have lost their moorings at home.

As much as they possess in the way of material things, relatively affluent children often lack what they need most: the presence of their parents. During the nearly two decades that I've been a practicing pediatrician, I've noticed a gradual but marked decline in the amount of time parents spend in truly meaningful encounters with their children.

One mother, who typifies many other parents I deal with, complained about one of the many caretakers who took care of her four-year-old son during the course of a week. It seems that the baby sitter had failed to report an earache, and now, the child was suffering from a fever and bad infection.

"I can't believe she let this thing go on for two whole days!" the mother said.

"Didn't *you* see your child during those two days?" I asked.

"Sure, but he was usually asleep; and besides, it's her job to keep on top of these things!"

As it happened, both the mother and the father had been under severe pressures at their respective jobs during the past week or two. They had been working such long hours that they had seen their child for only a few minutes during the last three mornings. Furthermore, for the past three nights they hadn't been with him at all, except to look in on him while he slept.

This husband and wife made quite a comfortable income between them. They belonged to the best clubs and, in general, were able to afford whatever they wanted. Their child was also a beneficiary of the largesse; he received so many toys that the overflow regularly had to be stored at the family's vacation home. But what the parents had failed to give their son was themselves and their time.

He was picked up by a sitter in the morning and taken to an all-day kindergarten. Then, he was picked up by the sitter at the end of the day and shuttled off to Suzuki violin lessons or some other scheduled activity. Several days a week, the sitter would be the one who saw that he went to sleep while the parents finished up their office work. The child had been moving around so quickly from one activity to the next that no adults had focused on the fact that his physical health was in jeopardy.

In part, the decline in child-parent contact typified by this case may be due to the increase in dual-career couples and single-parent families, whose long hours at the office keep parents away from home. And in part, the problem may arise from a tendency of both parents and children to get caught up in a fast-paced lifestyle.

But whatever the cause, there's no doubt that negative social and economic forces are at work, splitting children and their parents apart. Consider just a few pertinent trends.

Almost 46 percent of all couples with one or more children involve two working spouses, according to the U.S. Census Bureau.

More than 60 percent of mothers with children under fourteen—and that includes both single and married mothers—are in the labor force.

Many children are with caretakers other than their parents during most of the day. Specifically, 37 percent of American working women, with children under five years of age, arrange for child care in another home; 31 percent arrange for care in their own homes; and 23 percent put their children in organized child-care facilities. According to some estimates, nearly ten million preschoolers now spend their days with caretakers other than their parents.

Children in all-day programs account for about one-third of all pupils enrolled in the nation's kindergarten programs. That amounts to more than a million five- and six-year-olds who are in the care of people other than their parents most of the day.

The U.S. Census Bureau reports that about one-quarter of all American children now live with only one parent. Also, the bureau estimates that approximately two-thirds of all children will, at some time before they become adults, live in single-parent households.

The phenomenon of "latchkey children" has developed into a major national issue in recent years. These are the estimated 5 to 10 million children who spend some time during the day alone and unsupervised at home.

The problems associated with these children are numerous. A Louis Harris survey of teachers in 1987 revealed that the lack of after-school supervision was the primary cause of poor school performance. Parents questioned separately for the study showed that 41 percent left their children alone at least once a week between the end of school and 5:30 P.M. Nearly 25 percent of the parents left the children alone every day.

In another study—conducted by researchers at Johns Hopkins Children's Center and the University of Arizona—70 percent of latchkey children, aged five to thirteen, complained of being lonely or bored. Small percentages also said they were worried about their health and fearful of being alone in a house.

Whatever the circumstances or the reasons for the lack of interaction between parents and children, the results are disturbing. As we've already seen, schoolwork can suffer, and feelings of loneliness, boredom, and a variety of fears may plague children. Children often feel unwanted, even when the mother or father showers them with material goods or other seeming "advantages."

These children may adopt unusual and frequently unhealthy eating practices, abuse drugs, become depressed, lose self-esteem, and develop a host of other physical and emotional problems— problems that medical professionals like myself must ultimately try to sort out. In addition, there's a tendency in these children to hide their feelings and activities and to learn to lie to adults.

In hours and minutes, how much time do most parents actually spend with their children? A definitive work on this subject hasn't been conducted as yet. But some disquieting indicators are emerging in the research.

According to a study by the Institute for Social Research of the University of Michigan, mothers who work spent an average of only eleven minutes each day during the week in meaningful activities with their children and only thirty minutes a day on weekends. Fathers who work spent even fewer minutes with their children: eight minutes a day during the week, and fourteen minutes a day on weekends.

For purposes of the study, the researchers assumed that meaningful activities, which would qualify as "time spent with children," had to involve some sort of significant personal interaction. So, the investigators counted time spent talking with sons and daughters, actively playing with them, or reading to them. But just sitting in the child's presence without interaction—such as silently watching television—didn't count.

Affluenza Factor #2: Children are seen by adults as commodities.

Children who *seem* to have a great deal, but then fail in some way to take advantage of their apparent blessings, may stumble because they somehow get the message from their parents or other respected adults that they are something less than human. Their self-esteem is so low that they lack the inner resources to reach their full potential in life.

The problem may start at the very beginning, when prospective parents begin to analyze the costs of having a child. Consider what one father of a little seven-year-old girl, Sarah, told me in the youngster's presence during one of her regular checkups.

He said, "My wife and I have been thinking about having another kid, but do you realize what they cost these days? I was just reading in the paper the other day that it costs more than quarter of a million dollars just to get the average child out of high school! Can you imagine if you add on private schools like Sarah attends and then an expensive college?"

I was embarrassed for Sarah because she obviously became rather uncomfortable during the conversation. I doubt that she understood the full import of the dollar figures her father was tossing around. But she certainly got the message that money was a consideration in having her as well as the possible sibling.

Too often, this sort of thinking carries over into the child's upbringing. The youngster is regarded as a purchase or an investment, and heaven help whoever is responsible if there isn't a significant payoff in the end for all the money that has been spent!

One couple in New York City took this to something of an extreme after the wife underwent an unsuccessful sterilization operation. She conceived her fourth child after the operation and then promptly sued to recover $85,000, the estimated cost of raising the unwanted youngster.

David B. Wilson, a columnist for the *Boston Globe,* sums up this problem as well as anyone:

> Children, as a practical matter, have become consumer goods.
> And the implications of this change are, literally, awful. . . . As a con-
> sumer good, a child is, coldly analyzed, a marketing disaster.
>   The cost of obstetrics . . . dentistry, housing, tuition . . . and
> forfeited leisure is, at a guess, adequate funding for annual vacations
> abroad for two in each of the approximately two decades during
> which your utility-grade child is dependent on its parents for these
> goods and services. . . .
>   So when the choice is a baby or a BMW, the baby is likely to be
> postponed, if not cancelled outright. At least, a used BMW can be
> traded in on a new one.[1]

Day care for children is also a commodity, and good quality
day care is expensive. It's my impression that, many times, parents
consider day care a kind of "service contract" or "cost of doing business" with their child. Perhaps it would be better to consider day
care in terms of the impact it would have on their child's development.

Affluenza Factor #3: Children are deteriorating physically.

One day recently I saw four children in a row—two boys and
two girls, ranging in age from seven to fourteen. And they all had the
same problem: They were obese! Each had a sizable extra roll of fat
around the waist and weighed at least 10 percent more than he or she
should have.

Those children were specific examples of a widespread problem
of overweight, out-of-shape youngsters. There was a 54 percent increase in obesity among children six to eleven years old from 1963 to
1980, according to researchers at the Harvard School of Public
Health. This study, which was based on data from nearly twenty-
two thousand children, also revealed a 39 percent increase in obesity
among adolescents twelve to seventeen years old.

"Childhood obesity is epidemic in the United States," observed
Dr. William H. Dietz, Jr., a co-author of the study. The extra weight
and poor physical fitness contribute to lethargy, lack of stamina, and
various cardiovascular problems later in life.

What's causing this tendency to be overweight and out of
shape? The consumption of junk food and high-fat foods is certainly
one factor, and huge numbers of children have plenty of pocket
change available to indulge themselves. The average child consumes

at least the national average of about 40 percent of his total calories in the form of fats, even though the American Heart Association recommends that 30 percent or less of the daily intake of calories be in the form of fat.

Another reason for obesity is a lack of physical exercise—a fact that has been confirmed by various investigations. For example, the President's Council on Physical Fitness and Sports reported in 1987 that 40 percent of boys from age six to twelve, and 70 percent of girls from age six to seventeen, were unable to do more than one pull-up. Also, 33 percent of the boys and 50 percent of the girls couldn't run a mile in less than ten minutes. Physical fitness is so poor among the nation's youngsters that only 2 percent of the eighteen million who took the council's test performed well enough to qualify for the basic award!

Why aren't our children getting out and working off those extra pounds? A major reason is that we've provided them with attractive indoor alternatives, especially the wide variety of offerings on their TV sets, home video games, and movies for VCRs.

Children between the ages of two and twelve watch an average of twenty-five hours of television each week, according to research done by the American Academy of Pediatrics. This means that by the time he graduates from high school at about eighteen years of age, the average American child will have spent fifteen thousand hours in front of a TV set and will have seen about 350,000 commercials!

In comparison, this same "average child" will spend only about eleven thousand hours in a conventional classroom. Clearly, the major "school" that is instructing our children is the TV tube, with its questionable programming and hard-selling advertisements. Consequently, the values of many children begin to reflect the materialistic, chaotic, unsystematic presentations of the mass media rather than the firm, traditional values that once were the prerogative of the family.

On the physical front, there is plenty of evidence that television is a major culprit in promoting the deterioration of children's health. One study at Auburn University has shown that fitness levels decrease as television watching increases. Another study at the Harvard School of Public Health indicated that obesity increases 2 percent for each additional hour that a child spends in front of the television set each day. Only 10 percent of teenagers who watch an hour or less of

TV a day are obese, as compared with 20 percent of those who watch more than five hours daily.

Unfortunately, the future outlook for this couch-potato problem isn't too bright. Increased numbers of divorces and the rise of single-parent homes have caused television to become more of a baby sitter than ever before, one television executive from Lorimar Telepictures has observed. As a result, eight-year-olds are beginning to behave like twelve-year-olds. A Yankelovich Clancy Shulman survey found that more than one-third of nine- to eleven-year-old girls use deodorant, perfume, and nail polish regularly.

Still, there may be at least one ray of hope on the horizon. A survey by the Association of Independent Television Stations has found that 30 percent of the children questioned said they were bored by afternoon television. So instead of watching regular programming, they had turned to video tapes. In fact, the recent ratings of just one of the networks, ABC, have shown a viewership drop of 37 percent in children under the age of six.

Such drops translate into big bucks for the networks. The bible of the advertising world, *Advertising Age* magazine, has estimated that under current conditions, the three major networks may lose $40 million or more annually in commercial time because of lower children's ratings.

But let's not begin to cheer just yet. This slippage in regular television viewing may be significant for ad dollars, but it's not necessarily a step in the right direction for the children. Many of them simply exchange one couch-potato lifestyle for another. They may watch cable shows instead of network programs or stay glued to video tapes instead of cable shows or play video games instead of video tapes. Unfortunately, however, too few are turning to active, athletic pursuits that will enhance their health and physical well-being.

Finally, before we leave this topic, it's important to consider the other side of the coin. Although many children are overweight, many others, especially young girls, are obsessed with becoming thin. I see girls as young as nine or ten years old who have become preoccupied with their weight. Influenced by their mothers, older sisters, and the images seen daily on their TV screens, they are determined to take off every extra pound.

One very thin nine-year-old girl told me, "I'll never fit into my new bathing suit this summer if I don't watch my diet!" I'm virtually certain she had picked up this attitude from something her mother had said to the girl's overweight teenage sister.

A study published in the journal *Pediatrics* revealed that by age seven, children have already adopted prevailing adult perceptions of physical attractiveness, including attitudes toward weight. Eating disorders like anorexia nervosa have been identified in girls as young as ten. Finally, the study reported that half the girls interviewed thought they were too fat, even though 83 percent were normal in weight according to prevailing medical standards.

Clearly, as much as our children have in some ways, they're not getting the guidance and information they need to maintain basic levels of good health and fitness.

Some health-conscious parents may also retard their infants' development by forcing them to eat low-calorie, low-fat diets too early, the American Academy of Pediatrics has reported. This study stated that seven infants (aged seven to twenty-two months) in a Long Island hospital were "failing to thrive"—a syndrome that involves inadequate growth and delayed development. The cause of the problem: The college-educated parents were intent on imposing their health and nutrition philosophies on the babies, believing they were helping their children, when the practices were actually harmful to the babies' health.

Affluenza Factor #4: Too many children are emotionally unhealthy.

I find myself counseling increasing numbers of children about various emotional and psychosomatic problems. In a typical week, I'll have to deal with children

- ▶ who are depressed;
- ▶ who display various emotional symptoms of stress, such as nervousness, anger, insomnia, or too-frequent nightmares;
- ▶ who overeat because of the daily pressures they're under;
- ▶ who experience aches and pains, fatigue, nausea, or other physical problems, which result directly from emotional upsets they're facing; and

▶ who have developed an inordinate number of debilitating, immobilizing fears, such as a fear of going to school.

This problem of emotional difficulties among young people has become so severe that the American Academy of Pediatrics has decided to issue guidelines to encourage pediatricians to check the emotional as well as the physical state of their patients. So, instead of just asking where she hurts, a physician may ask Janice how well she gets along with other children or how she likes day care.

These guidelines are quite relevant and helpful these days because an estimated one in every eight American children—about 7.5 million in all—suffers from a mental health problem severe enough to require treatment, according to the Congressional Office of Technology. Unfortunately, 70 to 80 percent of these emotionally needy children aren't getting appropriate treatment, some because of a lack of money, and some because their well-heeled parents aren't attuned to the children's mental states.

Objectively speaking, many adults acknowledge that the challenges facing contemporary children are more severe than in years past. A poll by Louis Harris in 1986 revealed that three-fourths of adults think that children today face more problems than they did when they were growing up. Also, less than half of all adults believe most American children are basically happy. Furthermore, only about half feel that most children have loving parents.

A majority of adults feel so strongly about these problems that they say they are willing to put their money on the line to help solve them. If asked, they say, they would actually pay higher taxes for programs to combat drugs and to improve public schools, day-care facilities, and parks and recreation programs!

That may be what adults, including many parents, are willing to do on the broad political level. But when it comes to dealing with the unhappiness or emotional disturbances of individual children, the situation can get stickier.

The frustrated parents of one eight-year-old boy contacted me because their son frequently refused to attend school. "It's a major hassle getting him on the school bus in the morning," the father said. "He screams and yells, and we have to threaten him with a loss of television or some other punishment practically every day. Also, at least a couple of days a week, he'll check in to see the school nurse, complaining of a headache or a stomachache."

The father and mother were particularly annoyed and upset about the situation because they both were quite busy people. The father, who worked full-time, was regarded as being on a fast track for future promotions; so he frequently worked ten-hour days at the office. As for the mother, she held down a part-time job and had a "full plate" during the rest of the week with volunteer activities.

These parents had arranged various extracurricular classes and activities for their son. Also, they focused considerable attention on him and his interests during those limited hours when they were at home. Overall, they believed they were giving him every advantage.

But the child wasn't responding as they thought they had every right to expect. His problems were encroaching on their ability to concentrate and function on the job—that just didn't seem fair or acceptable.

These parents were by no means alone. As many as 10 percent of all school-age children are estimated to have school phobia at some point. In most cases, the problem can be relieved by parental reassurance and firmness. The key here is to open up a frank dialogue with the child so that he feels free to tell you how he feels about his fears. But it's important to clear up the difficulty as soon as possible because if these fears are allowed to fester, they may become more serious as the child gets older and may even spill over into adulthood.

Unfortunately, in the particular case that I was facing, the child had been wrestling with separation fears for years. He had started behaving this way during nursery school and had never grown out of it. As is often the case in such situations, the parents were quite loving and caring, and they had created a pleasant environment that the child didn't want to leave. Because they had encouraged him to become overly dependent on them—and because they couldn't always meet his need for their presence with the demands of their work and volunteer schedules—the boy's school phobia worsened over time.

The treatment required was family therapy and individual psychotherapy on a regular basis. Gradually, over a period of months, the boy developed more of an ability to deal with the school phobia problem, and his resistance to class attendance lessened. But he still remains vulnerable to these fears after Thanksgiving and Christmas vacations, when he has spent a particularly pleasant time at home with his parents.

What lessons can we learn from this family? Certainly, the parents have done well to be loving and concerned for their child when they are around him. Many children might respond quite differently to the same circumstances than has their son; they might develop an independence that would allow them to go about their own business, much as the parents go about theirs.

But this little boy is more vulnerable to school and separation fears than most, and the parents must accommodate his special needs. Alert parents can often identify incipient problems and phobias like this by talking with other parents or child-care professionals and then making comparisons with their own son or daughter.

As I've said, it's best to act early, at the very first signs of difficulty. Many times, a little more attention by the parents—coupled with in-depth parent-child conversations and loving encouragement to become more independent—can set the fearful child on the right track. In the older child, however, this sort of separation anxiety may have to be treated through special therapy and, in a few cases, medication.

Affluenza Factor #5: Children have become too jaded.

A colleague of mine sighed at the end of a particularly tough day, "I think I've run into more jaded, worldly wise seven-year-olds in the past week than in any other week in my entire practice! The problem seems to be escalating."

He was referring to the fact that children these days seem to have acquired more, seen more, and done more than any past generation. And the age at which they are acquiring, seeing, and doing is getting younger and younger. Having such a surfeit of goods, services, and experiences often seems to take some of the wonder and innocence out of childhood and hastens the onset of a hollow, materialistic set of values that characterizes so many adults in our society.

In this regard, I'm reminded of a 1985 study done by *The Wall Street Journal* and the Gallup group that looked into the impact of the "good life" on children of top business executives. The young people, aged fourteen to twenty-two, lived in the lap of luxury and comfort, and their preferences and values were shaped by their material advantages. More than half the young people cited material or financial advantages as the best part of being the child of a successful executive.

"I get the things I want," one survey respondent said. "I can go to the most expensive college in the country and not have to worry about it."

They don't have to worry about daily life and leisure, either: 75 percent have mothers who stay home to take them to riding and ballet lessons; 30 percent have swimming pools; and a large number enjoy country club memberships.

But the impact of worldly possessions and advantages doesn't always seem to yield productive or even entirely happy offspring. For one thing, the boys and girls don't seem to spend much time dreaming about ways to change society for the better or to apply their energies to high-flown creative pursuits—at least not unless those pursuits produce money. The most popular occupations they envisage include those that pay high salaries: 20 percent want to go into business; 8 percent want to be engineers; 6 percent plan to become physicians; and 5 percent want to be lawyers.

Yet their easy lives and money-oriented career ambitions don't necessarily result in personal satisfaction. In fact, the main pressures they feel are directly related to their affluence. They report (1) being uncomfortable being cast in the role of "rich kid" by their peers at school; (2) being regarded on occasion as a "spoiled brat"; (3) sensing that their parents sometimes try to buy their love with material things; (4) feeling pressure from their parents to achieve; and (5) having too little time with their hard-working, often-absent dads.

These affluenza factors provide an introduction to the forces underlying what I've identified as the Rich Kids Syndrome. Sometimes, the syndrome afflicts children and families who really are quite wealthy. But more often, the problem creeps into the lives of those who are merely well-off, who are comfortably middle-class, or who simply aspire to greater incomes, acquisitions, and status.

Unfortunately, the ones who suffer the most emotional and

physical problems from the syndrome are the children who are thrust into home situations and relationships that they didn't create. Their parents, consciously or inadvertently, provide them with too much of one thing or another, and the children pay the consequences. Ironically, some of the most serious victims of the syndrome are those youngsters who have too much of what almost everyone assumes is an unadulterated blessing—freedom.

Chapter Three

Kids Who Have Too Much Freedom

For months, the pall of the "preppie" murder case hung heavily over the Manhattan social scene. The circumstances just hit too close to home for many of the affluent, well-educated, and well-meaning parents of New York City. In the posh apartments and townhouses of the fashionable Upper East Side, mothers and fathers pondered the reports in the news media and often found themselves desperately trying to distinguish *their* family from the unfortunate family of the accused nineteen-year-old killer, Robert Chambers.

The disturbing facts, as they gradually emerged over the months, were grim and hard to grasp. On a sultry night in August 1986, the handsome six-foot-four-inch Chambers—a former student at the exclusive Choate School in Connecticut and a graduate of a private preparatory school in Manhattan—walked into one of his hangouts, a trendy bar on the Upper East Side. There, he met Jennifer Levin, a tall, attractive eighteen-year-old who had just graduated from the Baldwin School. Levin carried a fake identification card because the minimum legal age to buy alcoholic beverages in New York is twenty-one.

After some talking and drinking, the two left the bar together and headed for Central Park, where they engaged in sexual activity during the early morning hours. At that point, things began to get ugly. According to a statement Chambers gave to the police, Levin hurt him during what might be called some "rough sex." He retaliated by grasping her by the neck—and she was strangled to death.

Chambers was indicted for murder and eventually pleaded guilty to manslaughter. In a plea-bargain arrangement, he was given a sentence of five to fifteen years in prison, with a minimum term of five years.

The startling thing about this tragic case for many upper-middle-class people was not so much that a terrible murder had been committed, but that, as one executive said, "It involved people like us!"

As the facts were published in the papers, the points of identification came eerily close to the lives of more than one well-heeled urban family. Both Jennifer Levin and Robert Chambers were children of divorce, as are many other affluent youngsters. Also, they exercised tremendous freedom and control over their lives, with much of their time in the evenings being spent as underage drinkers in chic Manhattan "watering holes." In their set, money was no obstacle; credit cards were omnipresent; and they had plenty of idle time and opportunity to engage in drug and alcohol use and sexual activity.

By most standards, children like these are regarded as "privileged"; they have been "given every opportunity," including a good education and practically any material thing they desire. All things considered, they seem to have a bright, unlimited future. But somehow, all these "privileges" and "opportunities" aren't enough. Something essential seems to be missing, something that can make the difference between happiness and anguish, success and failure, a productive life and a wasted one.

Clearly, in the case of Chambers and Levin something went *drastically* wrong. Other parents in similar circumstances—attempting to analyze and draw useful lessons from the tragedy of this boy and girl—began to do some serious soul-searching. It was the same kind of ruminating that you may do about yourself sometimes when you read about a crime in your neighborhood. Perhaps you wonder, "What can I do to avoid this danger myself? Have I taken sufficient protective steps? Or should I change my life and habits in some way to lower my risks?"

The unnerving thing about the Chambers-Levin affair was that no easy solutions or answers emerged. There seemed no obvious way for many upscale, affluent parents to distinguish that situation from their own. As Ronald P. Stewart, the headmaster of York Preparatory School put it: "Everyone is looking for some 'bad seed' thread in Robert Chambers, something to make us say, 'Aha, we should have known.' But the more worrying conclusion is that there are environmental factors. That there is a generation of students who may have lost their moral bearings. That parents are not parenting in the way they used to."

The root problem, in short, is that we have given our children too much freedom. We've told them when they are too young, "You have to become more independent. You must learn to operate on your own." To compound the problem, as we've cut them loose from the moorings of a secure home life, we haven't supplied them with adequate guidelines to live by. We have been too busy with our own lives or have been confused and vague about what to teach. Too few children have clear, reliable roadmaps based on meaningful values and rules of morality. They aren't taught appropriately at home what's right and what's wrong; instead, they are left to their own devices to find out the answer by themselves. Unfortunately, they often fail, sometimes with tragic results.

To understand how the freedom of children can get out of hand, I've identified some trends that I regard as basic causes of the problem. Let's first take a look at these causes, and then we'll consider some possible solutions.

How a Child Can Get Too Much Freedom

In my medical practice, as well as in my exposure to various other aspects of the family scene around the country, I've encountered at least five trends that give rise to an excessive, destructive kind of freedom for children.

Trend #1: A lack of moral certainty in parents.

In dealing with their children, many parents lack the certainty and decisiveness that accompany a strong set of moral values. Having strong values frequently means defending them and being accountable for them. In a fast-paced life, it's easier to avoid the energy required to choose and monitor the best moral values for families.

Furthermore, we live in a society where relativism has run rampant. In the view of many adults, one set of beliefs is as good as the next. It's up to each individual to make up his or her own mind about the moral or spiritual values to follow, and it really doesn't make much difference what approach the person takes.

This way of thinking also often becomes a part of the parents' child-rearing philosophy. The child is supposed to make up his own mind, with as little influence from the parent as possible. I frequently hear comments like these:

▶ "I've exposed my daughter to a variety of religious beliefs so that she can make an intelligent decision when she gets older."
▶ "I try not to impose my personal moral beliefs on my son. He's got to develop his own philosophy and live his own life."
▶ "I don't care what my child believes as long as he's happy."
▶ "I haven't been too dogmatic in teaching my children about moral values because they may reject mine and have none."
▶ "What if the values I affirm are of no use to my son, because many of my parents' values don't seem relevant now?"

Yet it seems to me that such attitudes represent a serious abdication of parental responsibility. If you're going to provide a child with a good education, good health, a good camping experience, good music lessons—and perhaps a good automobile—why not give him a good set of personal values as well?

This question is by no means an abstract or academic one, either. The parents of one teenage boy seen in my practice got divorced when he was eight. The parents had joint custody, and apparently competing for the title of "best parent," they spared him very little in material benefits. Both parents were wary of trying to discipline the boy too firmly or "lay down the law" about his social and academic life. As a result, the youngster, though quite intelligent, consistently underachieved at his private school; he regularly made *C*'s and *D*'s instead of the *A*'s and *B*'s he was capable of.

Also, he indulged in mild drug use and occasional use of alcohol, primarily because he had far too much money. His parents always gave him a generous allowance, apparently in an effort to buy his love. Soon, the boy was involved in regular sexual relationships with some of his female classmates, and before long, he contracted genital herpes.

What we have here is a youngster who got off to a very bad start in life, mainly because his parents gave him too much freedom and not enough solid adult guidance. They always said, "Those teachers of his don't do a thing to help him in his studies!" Yet the parents completely overlooked the fact that as his primary caretakers, *they* had the major responsibility to help the boy learn proper discipline and wise use of his freedom and advantages.

It took several months of therapy for these parents and their son to begin to understand and accept what was going wrong. But even when the parents did finally start to acknowledge their responsibility in the matter, they found it was difficult, uphill going. The fact that the mother and father were living apart didn't help matters. Moreover, it wasn't easy to try to correct the years of abused freedom their boy had become accustomed to. How do you tell a son who is practically an adult, "You should believe this" or "You should do that," when previously there has been no such strong guidance?

This boy was almost ready to leave home and launch an independent life. He had already started applying to colleges, and his personality, moral values, and aspirations had already been firmly shaped—though often not in the direction his parents would have preferred.

Finally, he did make some progress in pulling his life together. For example, because of his unfortunate experience with a sexually transmitted disease, he recognized that it would be wise to be wary of unbridled sexual expression in the future. Also, he acknowledged that his parents were right in their warnings about drug use. Two of his friends had recently been victims of overdoses.

But as of this writing, he still has a long way to go in overcoming the negative effects of the excessive freedom he had experienced for so long. He's a prime example of how too much freedom—with no strong parental guidance about personal values—can cause a young person to court disaster.

I've discovered that in most cases, children ask—indeed, *beg*—for moral and spiritual guidance from their parents. One girl with this problem went away to college but soon ran into many problems adjusting to the new environment. A major source of her difficulties was that her parents assumed that she was more of an adult than she really was, and out of their ignorance, they refused to give her the parental guidance she desperately needed.

Many times, when this girl called Mom and Dad for advice, they would cut the conversation short by saying something like this:

"Well, you're on your own now. You'll have to evaluate these situations and make your own decisions."

Such responses, though well-intentioned, drove the daughter to tears more than once. To make matters worse, the parents had showered material possessions on her—possessions that she wasn't equipped to manage properly.

For example, they had bought the girl a condominium in the university town where she was living rather than encourage her to live in a dormitory. As a result, she found herself quite isolated from many of the other students, and she had considerable trouble developing a meaningful social life.

If this girl had been a naturally gregarious, mature young person, she might have overcome her living situation; she might even have used it to her advantage. But instead, she found herself spending most of her time alone, surrounded by her many possessions. Soon, she began to display various signs of stress, including headaches, gastrointestinal problems, and irritability. Later, she became depressed and failed to attend classes because of her overwhelming fatigue.

Finally, the family sought some psychological and medical advice. They were told to let their eighteen-year-old grow up with more appropriate assistance in choosing and testing her values. And that meant allowing her to ease more gradually out of childhood and into adulthood. The main idea was not to try to turn her into a completely independent person before she was ready. She was obviously still in a transition stage between dependence on her mother and father and the freedom of mature adulthood.

One practical part of the solution was to move her into a dormitory. There, life was more predictable and structured, with more opportunities to form friendships. Also, the parents became freer in communicating advice and guidance. These and other such measures helped this young woman to recover from the consequences of too much freedom.

To sum up, then, parents *must* become bolder in transmitting their own values to their children. Obviously, the mother or father without a well-formed set of values is in no position to teach children in this important area. So for some parents, an important first step will be to examine their own positions on right and wrong, good and evil—and then to take a stand.

But after a commitment has been made to a personal moral and spiritual philosophy, there's an essential second step: Take the opportunity to teach your child the values you've acquired. When you reach this point, it's important not to be timid. It is your responsibility as a parent to impart moral values and a responsibility you shouldn't abdicate easily. Your hard-learned values can help your child. So be bold and begin to transmit those values that can make your youngster's experience of freedom a joy rather than a disaster.

Trend #2: Working parents.

Many children are acquiring freedom from adult supervision as a direct result of having their parents working at jobs outside the house. This condition is extremely widespread and seems to be growing. More than two-thirds of the mothers in the United States are working women, and about one-half of all American couples are two-career couples, according to the U.S. Labor Department.

In many cases, of course, it's economically necessary for both parents to hold down jobs. But that necessity doesn't eliminate the problems that may arise when both of them are absent for long periods.

One of my colleagues was the pediatrician for a four-year-old boy whose mother returned to work. When the boy came in for a checkup, he came across as a clearly unhappy youngster. The boy was well-dressed and seemed to have all the material advantages he could want. But he constantly whined and cried and chewed on his fingers while he was in the doctor's office. In general, he seemed more agitated than the average youngster.

The child-care situation around the home helped explain many of the problems. The boy's grandmother, who cared for him during the day, mostly catered to his every whim and frequently sided with him against the mother. The father, who worked full-time, didn't get involved in child care except for occasionally assisting the mother in putting the boy to bed.

During his conversations with the mother, the pediatrician discerned that she felt guilty and was compensating in various ways to make up for her absence from home. For example, when she was around the boy, she was constantly attentive to his physical needs and badgered him about eating all the right foods.

"Sometimes, I'm afraid he's going to starve to death. He seems to eat so little!" she said.

In fact, the boy was quite well-nourished. But the mother was unable to look at him objectively because of those guilt feelings. She somehow felt she had to be overly attentive to him in order to assuage her own feelings of having fallen short as a parent. Basic to the mother's feelings was her ambivalence about her desire to return to her career.

The boy, for his part, seemed angry that his mother had to be gone from home so much. He had gotten used to her presence around the home, and he seemed to feel that by acting up and manipulating her with his whining and complaining, he could somehow bring her back home to stay. Interestingly enough, the boy accepted the fact that his father had to be away from home at work all day because he had never known anything else.

This was a situation where there were no rules for the child to operate under—no requirements about what to eat, when to eat, or how to behave in other ways. Tantrums were accepted as a matter of course, as though they were perfectly justified and entirely the fault of the mother.

What was needed here—and what the doctor recommended— was the establishment and enforcement of rules of conduct for the child in the home. Also, both his grandmother and his mother had to adhere to the same rules. His excessive freedom, while in the care of his grandmother during the day and of his mother at night, had placed an undue burden on him. No preschooler is capable of running his own life. He was *crying out* to be told consistently what to do, and he needed to know the consequences if he didn't comply.

I'm all for positive reinforcement of good behavior and for maintaining a positive, upbeat atmosphere in the home. Heavy-handed punishment doesn't work over the long haul to instill proper values and actions in a child. But in the last analysis, there has to be a bottom line. There has to be a point where the parent makes it clear: "Your freedom is limited. These are the outside boundaries, and you have to operate within them." Children want and need this type of message, and parents—including working parents who may feel somewhat guilty about their absence from the home—must have the courage to communicate it.

Trend #3: Single parents.

Another tendency that often promotes too much of the wrong kind of freedom for children is the increase in single-parent homes. About one-fourth of all American families are currently run by single parents, according to the U.S. Bureau of Labor Statistics. Furthermore, an estimated two-thirds of today's newborn children will spend some time growing up in a single-parent home.

It stands to reason that when there are two parents instead of one, the child will probably get more attention and guidance, even if the second parent is relatively uninvolved. These days, an increasing number of fathers in two-parent families whom I encounter in my practice do get involved with their children. Even where that's not the case—where a father takes a hands-off attitude toward child-rearing—most of these dads will respond when the mother gets completely exasperated and demands some help.

With single parents, however, no such last-ditch demand is possible, simply because there's no other spouse to rely on in a pinch. This situation can create major pressures for mothers (who comprise about 90 percent of all single parents) and also for many fathers who are on their own.

A female partner in a large New York law firm tried to adjust her job requirements so that she could devote more time to being a single parent. She cut down on her time spent at the office and also on cases that required travel.

But still, she was forced into a juggling act. On one occasion, she had to call in her parents from out of state on an emergency basis to take care of her child while she worked on a case. Another time, feeling she wasn't spending enough time with the youngster, she brought him to work during what seemed a lull in her responsibilities. But she was called away unexpectedly and had to leave the child in the care of paralegals until she returned.

"I felt really guilty," she said. "It wasn't a professional thing to do."

What if the situation arose again—could she say no to the demands of the job? "I don't know," she replied. "Chances are, I wouldn't."[1]

As far as the children in such situations are concerned, being on their own while the single parent is at work can produce stresses. A woman who was a top-level, ten–hour-a-day manager of a large service corporation reported that her daughter was having problems due to her frequent absences.

She said, "I'd love to be able to say my daughter is a lovely, well-adjusted child, but she's not. She's very much of a monster." The girl is given to temper tantrums and rebellious behavior—a result, this parent believes, of too little mothering.

This mother's greatest worry is that one day, the daughter will say, "I wish you'd been there for me, Mother."

Trend #4: Divorce.

The incredible number of divorces that occur every year leaves families in a state of social shipwreck, with children afloat on a tempestous, confusing moral sea, tossed to and fro by conflicting directions and influences. Mothers and fathers of more than one million children get divorced every year, and by some estimates, 40 percent of children born today run the risk of experiencing a family divorce.

When I see various patients—whose damaged lives bring these statistics to life—I sometimes wonder whether parents really consider how their actions are wreaking havoc on their children. Several years ago, one well-to-do husband and wife with a nine-year-old boy underwent a particularly acrimonious divorce; after long and bitter legal proceedings, they agreed on joint custody. Specifically, it was agreed that the boy would live with his mother during the school year; his father would have custody on weekends, school vacations, and summer vacation.

Despite the fight they engaged in over the child, neither really had much time for him. Both parents were carrying on high-powered careers, and no matter which one he happened to be staying with, his primary caretaker was a baby sitter. It became apparent in conversations with them that their custody battles hadn't really been as much about the boy as about their desire to settle old scores with each other.

The impact of the divorce and its aftermath on the child were quite destructive. He was given a tremendous amount of freedom in some ways. For example, he walked to his private school by himself. The daily trek took him through a large urban area along streets where drug dealing, prostitution, and heavy auto traffic were common. Also, his mother's baby sitter doubled as a maid, and she spoke heavily accented English. She had little time or inclination to interact verbally with the boy, and she encouraged him to operate on his own as much as possible.

The result of all this was that instead of developing a healthy independence, the youngster became fearful and extremely nervous. As he sat in my office, I could see his eyes darting back and forth, taking in the surroundings like a wild young animal who felt he might have to fend off danger at any moment.

Also, the boy was starved for attention. He spent a great deal of time by himself because there were no adults to interact with him, and it was a major undertaking to set up play dates with other children. For one thing, the baby sitter didn't want to bother with handling other children, and neither parent had taken time to analyze the boy's situation to see whether he needed more peer involvement. Also, when an infrequent play date opportunity did arise, other children's parents were reluctant to have their children visit the boy because of the lack of adult supervision.

In an effort to get the attention he desperately craved, he began to "act up" at school, sometimes in bizarre ways. On several occasions, for instance, he tossed his food at other children in the lunchroom; another time, he brought a roll of toilet paper into the classroom from the school bathroom in order to get a laugh. Also, he was quick to pick fights on the playground.

As he had intended, such antics made his classmates sit up and take notice, but they also caused his teachers to label him a troublemaker. "Is there something physically wrong with this boy, Dr. Minear?" his mother asked. "He seems so nervous and just doesn't act like most other children."

After a series of tests, I assured her that the youngster was completely healthy physically, but his emotional state was another matter. He was eventually referred to a family therapist, along with his mother and father. The problem wasn't really the boy's; it had been created by the interactions of the parents with the child. The best approach for them was to work out the situation together.

Unfortunately, the therapy sessions didn't continue long enough because neither parent could find the time for them. Still, there had been improvement, and to continue the gains, the parents wanted the boy to be seen alone by the psychologist. But this was unacceptable from the viewpoint of adequate treatment. Again, he was to be cut loose from parental involvement and cast out into life on his own, with only a therapist to give him some advice once or twice a week. Such parental behavior just barely misses the classification of neglect under the intent of many child protection laws.

The boy's plight was typical of many affluent children: too much of the wrong kind of freedom, too little of the right kind of parental influence. Even plans to have a stronger involvement by his school counselor were interrupted by a move to a neighboring community.

At last report from his new pediatrician, this boy had slipped backward. His academic performance at school was average at best; he was continuing to have disciplinary problems; and he periodically developed vague physical complaints and stomach upsets, which can be attributed only to the stresses bearing down on him. He needs loving, consistent parental involvement; instead, he receives a turned back. This situation reminds one of Jesus' rhetorical question to His disciples: "If a son asks for bread from any father among you, will he give him a stone? Or if he asks for a fish, will he give him a serpent instead of a fish? Or if he asks for an egg, will he offer him a scorpion?" (Luke 11:11–12). Clearly, some parents today dispense the wrong things to their children.

Unless something changes drastically, this young boy—who has all the material things and advantages that money can buy—will end up achieving at a level far below his potential. And he will eventually become an unhappy, disturbed adult.

In some ways, this family's dilemma serves as a classic illustration of the 1988 report by the Center for Family in Transition at Corte Madera, California. The center studied the impact of joint custody on children and concluded that the arrangement can be a mixed bag, at best.

The findings indicated that when divorces are bitter, joint custody seems to be worse for the child than single-parent custody. When divorces are relatively friendly and peaceful, joint custody seems to have about the same impact on the child as single-parent custody. More important than any custody arrangement, however, are these factors: (1) the quality of interactions with caring adults; (2) the age and sex of the child when the divorce occurs (younger children and boys have the hardest time adjusting); (3) the level of conflict between the parents (the less conflict, the better for the child); and (4) the psychological state of the parents (well-adjusted parents tend to have children with fewer emotional problems; parents with high levels of anxiety or depression have children with more problems).

Trend #5: Child care.

Obviously, many of these trends, which lead to excessive freedom for a child, are related to one another, and the movement toward more child care is no exception. Parents rely on sitters or services because of many of the factors already described: divorce, single parenthood, dual-career marriages.

The statistics are staggering. In the first place, more than half the women who have a baby return to work or actively begin to seek work within a year of having their babies. About 10.5 million children younger than six have mothers in the labor force, and most of these youngsters are cared for outside the home. In many cases, these children are taken care of in groups, where the individual boys and girls get less adult attention than those in one-to-one relationships with their caretakers. In short, children being cared for by surrogates frequently are left to their own devices more than those who are constantly interacting with a special adult. So increased reliance on child care is an important trend that needs to be considered as a source of uncontrolled independence.

A sizable majority of the children I see are in the care of surrogate caretakers for several hours each week. In many cases, the children spend more time with baby sitters or in child care than they do with their parents.

This trend has the potential for many unwanted outcomes. I believe that the interests of the child are best served by the child's being with a parent as much as possible in a consistent, regular time frame. In general, I urge parents to place as much priority for being with their child as for any other activity, including making money.

There's no doubt that child-care arrangements are a necessity in many, many families these days. But somehow, parents in this situation must fight to spend adequate time with their child. Otherwise, they won't be in a position to exercise sufficient influence and guidance over the child's development. A child without such parental control is placed at a serious disadvantage in dealing with challenges later in life.

One of the greatest problems I've observed in families with child–care surrogates is that the parents do not spend an appropriate amount of time defining and then finding the best sitter. Parental priorities often come across clearly when you raise the question of whether or not a certain kind of child care is best for a boy or girl.

One young working mother, a professional with heavy career responsibilities, blurted to me, "I didn't spend years in college and graduate school preparing for a career just to stop work and take care of a child!"

In fact, I hadn't suggested that she stop work—just that she re-evaluate the arrangement she and her husband had established for their two children. But this young mother hadn't prepared nearly as well for her children's welfare as she had for her career. Consider what she and her husband had done and left undone.

They were paying "an arm and a leg" for a full-time sitter, as the husband put it. But they had spent only about twenty minutes interviewing the woman and had received her references without bothering to check them thoroughly. They were so busy that when they couldn't immediately reach two of the references by phone, they charged ahead and hired the woman anyway.

English was not the sitter's first language, and she was unfamiliar with their neighborhood and with their children's school routines. On more than one occasion the children were left on the front steps by a neighbor or bus driver unable to get into the house. Also, it was clear to me that the children weren't getting adequate intellectual stimulation or conversational development, which was a predictable outcome because they couldn't communicate well with their sitter, who was the adult with them most of each day.

These difficulties almost resulted in a serious health problem when their three-year-old daughter developed fever, nausea, and stomachache. The mother brought the child to me early one morning, saying, "I think this child had a fever yesterday—at least, that's what the baby sitter told me. But she was asleep when I got home last night, so I wasn't able to tell exactly what was wrong."

The baby sitter had been with the child all day and supposedly had been observing the signs of the illness. But somehow she and the parents had failed to talk about the child's behavior and symptoms in any detail. In addition, there was no plan to routinely report unusual events to the parents each day. We unfortunately didn't have the sitter there with us to explain what she had seen.

It always helps a doctor in making a diagnosis in a case like this to know whether a child has had diarrhea, has been coughing, or has an inability to hold urine or a burning when voiding urine. As for the little girl, she couldn't describe what was wrong other than to say she was sick and her stomach hurt. She and her brother had, in effect, been put in charge of their own health, and of course, they were too young to recognize when something serious might be wrong with them. I had to start at square one in figuring out what was wrong with the girl.

After performing an exam and running some laboratory tests, I discovered that the youngster had a bacterial infection of the urinary tract—a condition that required an antibiotic over a period of about fourteen days with a follow-up exam and more tests. Fortunately, we caught the condition early enough so that the infection could be cleared up without any complications. But I told the parents rather sternly that they *had* to establish better lines of communication with their sitter if they wanted to ensure their children's health and safety in the future.

A more ominous set of problems with child care arises when child abuse rears its ugly head. If parents check out a sitter or child-care facility thoroughly, they can reduce the risk of this problem. But still, physical, psychological, and sexual abuse are issues that moms and dads must always be alert to when someone else is spending most of the day with their children.

One little four-year-old girl who was brought to me for an exam balked when she was asked by her mother to undress. "I'm not going to take off my clothes," she cried. "He's not going to touch me down there, is he?"

This reaction surprised me because the child had a cough but no other complaints that might have indicated an abuse problem. As we chatted further, I learned that she had been attending a day-care center while her mother, a single parent, was at work. As it turned out, the people running the day-care center hadn't perpetrated the abuse, but there *was* a problem with some of the older boys who attended the center. They had been fondling the child, and she hadn't developed an open enough relationship with her parents to be able to tell them about what was happening to her.

It's difficult for any child, no matter how close he or she is to a parent, to discuss sexual abuse. The child often has a sense that "I did something wrong," even though she isn't at fault at all. But this little girl had obviously had enough and wasn't going to put up with what she perceived as the same activity by an adult in her mother's very presence!

Problems like these are likely to increase in the future because of the tendency of working parents to rely on child care. According to the U.S. Census Bureau, 25 percent of American working women who have a child under age five used such facilities in 1985—up from 16 percent in 1982. An estimated $12 billion annually is spent on child care, but the services received don't always seem worth the cost. One in twenty working mothers told Census Bureau interviewers that she had lost time from work during the previous month because of child-care problems.

My advice to parents on day care and baby sitters can be summed up in two general pieces of advice. First, discuss appropriate amounts of time you expect to spend at work and in the care of your child with your employer. Creative work schedules often are available and can be negotiated. When there's a choice, always be your child's primary caretaker, but do so with positive conviction, not regrets. Second, screen and check your child-care person thoroughly. Prepare for child care in the same way you would prepare for the most important decision or project in your career.

In enumerating these trends, I'm not suggesting that every set of parents can eliminate the impact of these factors completely. Obviously, if you've already gone through a divorce, or if you're a single parent, you're dealing with a "given." You just have to make the best of the life situation in which you find yourself.

In addition, I want to convey a message of hope. No matter how difficult your circumstances, you can still expect good results. Indeed, many parents who seem to have practically everything going against them can do a wonderful job of helping their children to become productive, well-adjusted adults.

My purpose here has simply been to point out the possible sources of the problems your child may be facing with excessive freedom—and to begin to point toward some answers. Now, let's get even more specific and practical as we consider how you might identify and respond to some specific warning signs that too much freedom has crept into your child's life.

▶ *Chapter Four*

The Danger Signals of Too Much Freedom—and Practical Ways Parents Can Respond

---

In my practice, I've identified some key danger signals that indicate a child has too much freedom and needs more parental attention and guidance. Here are the main ones, with suggested responses to minimize or remove the danger.

Danger Signal #1: Evidence of smoking, alcohol consumption, or drug use.

This signal is so obvious that it may seem hardly worth mentioning. But I'm constantly appalled by the number of *very* young people who have become involved with tobacco, alcohol, or drugs. And many times, their parents don't regard their behavior as a particular problem.

A few of my ten- and eleven-year-old patients periodically smoke cigarettes. One twelve-year-old, who had telltale nicotine stains on his teeth, responded this way when I questioned him: "Sure, I smoke some. Most of my friends do. But my mom and dad don't worry about me. They say it's just a phase."

Others, when they reach junior high and high school, may get involved heavily with drugs, including alcohol. Among some would-be parental sophisticates, it's considered enlightened and liberal to allow young children to taste, and even imbibe rather heavily, wines and wine coolers.

"We don't let him drink regularly," one mother told me. "But on special occasions"—and that meant about once a week at dinner parties—"we pour Rob a drink along with everybody else. Otherwise, he feels left out."

Rob, incidentally, was twelve years old. This mother justified the practice with the argument, "The Europeans treat their children like adults, so why should we keep our son in a box? He'll be a more cultured person for the experience, and I'm sure he'll learn more about how to handle alcohol if we teach him at home rather than allow his education to take place on the outside."

In fact, Rob developed a serious drinking problem by the time he was fourteen. Contrary to his parents' expectations, he came to regard being able to drink a lot of liquor as a sign of being grown-up. But he was far too young to handle the experience, either emotionally or physically.

What's an appropriate approach for parents in a situation like this? Many parents fail to understand that children simply aren't ready to make intelligent, mature decisions about social use of drugs that alter their mental state and have the potential to be dangerous (addicting). First of all, their judgment is likely to be impaired too quickly due to the drug. Further, their life experiences are not varied enough to be useful in decision making.

Also, boys and girls in late elementary school, junior high, and high school are extremely vulnerable to peer pressures and influences. Of course, good peer groups, such as church, scouting, or athletic organizations, may discourage the use of substances that ultimately take control away from the adolescent. But if they've already had some experience with alcohol, drugs, or smoking, that may seem to place them in a more "advanced," "mature," or "street-smart" position in relation to their peers. They may be encouraged to go even deeper into substance abuse, and in the process, they may develop negative leadership traits that drag other youngsters down with them.

Then, there's the physical side of this problem. Because most of these children haven't grown to their full bodily stature or weight, it will take a much lower dose of alcohol or drugs to produce a significant or even lethal reaction in their bodies. If their main models are adults, some of whom are involved to one degree or another in substance abuse, the children may try to emulate the grown-up example—with disastrous results.

In light of these facts, my advice is rather straightforward. Beginning at an early age with the child, parents should discourage the use of harmful substances. Also, parents should discourage the implied "magic" of medicines to relieve pain, tension, and sleepless nights—contrary to the messages in much advertising. A child should be told in simple, easy-to-understand, *educational* terms what's wrong with drinking, smoking, and taking drugs. For example, in discussing newspaper or TV news stories and programs, a mother or father might say, "Did you see how that person lit up a cigarette and poured a drink in order to cope with the pain in that scene? That wasn't too smart. Can you think of other ways he could have faced the pain?"

"You see that man killed a boy with a car. It was because he was drinking alcohol. He wasn't in control of his actions because the alcohol got in the way."

"That person is going to jail because he was using and selling drugs. Getting involved with drugs is a punishable crime."

"Some people say that taking steroid drugs will make you a better athlete. But actually, steroids may just make you overly aggressive and belligerent. Also, with these substances in your system, you'll become more prone to injury because your muscles become too strong for your bones, tendons, and ligaments. These drugs can make you unhealthy in other ways, such as by upsetting the chemical balance in your body."

"You know Mr. Jones, who died the other day? He had lung cancer, and that disease comes as a direct result of his smoking."

This method of communication becomes important because a primary task of parents is to prepare and move their children toward independence.

Obviously, it's harder to get these points across if the parents use any of these substances. In fact, it's practically impossible to be a good example to your child about smoking or using drugs if you engage in these activities, though you may be able to convince the child that he should hold off on these activities until he gets older.

As far as alcohol is concerned, I'm *completely* opposed to the so-called European approach used by the parents in a previous example.

In other words, I don't think there's any justification for introducing children at a young age to limited wine or liquor use. As far as I can tell, there's no evidence to support the idea that such children will be taught how to handle it better when they get older. Some studies have found the incidence of youthful alcoholism and alcohol abuse to be exceptionally high in countries like France, which have been freer about introducing wine to children at a young age.

In my opinion, there's far too much of a risk with children who are given alcoholic drinks—such as a lick from the fingers or sips from spoons at very young ages, and then small glasses of wine by the time they are ten or twelve. This is an abuse rather than a wise use of freedom. I worry that such youngsters may be tempted to drink regularly while they're still in their important growing phase, and that could do irreparable damage to them.

On the other hand, there seem to be two other, more constructive schools of thought about drinking that may work to the child's advantage.

The first says, "Drinking in moderation is all right for adults, but it's totally unacceptable for children. If the parents become good role models for their youngsters—such as by strictly limiting their consumption around the home and never drinking when they're about to drive or engage in other activities that require alertness—the message will be more likely to get across."

Advocates of the second school of thought—to be sure, a more radical and less prevalent position than the first—state their case like this: "Drinking in any form is unnecessary and a bad example for a child. As a result, we're not going to drink at all, at least not while he's in the impressionable, youthful years."

Those who oppose this second point of view may argue that most people are eventually going to drink, and it's best to show them the right way rather than not to show them at all. But there seem to be no definitive studies on this subject. And individual case studies indicate this second approach, if handled wisely by parents, works at least as well as the first.

The key seems to be a loving, understanding, nonjudgmental approach to teaching the child. If parents are heavy-handed and provoke a child to rebel, the first things the youngster will typically choose to express that rebellion will be the behaviors that the parents have always discouraged or prohibited. So, if you say, "Don't smoke" or "You can't drink" or "I'd better not ever hear about you using drugs," you can bet that these activities will be the first the rebellious child gets involved in.

One mother and father took what turned out to be a more convincing approach for the child. They had been moderate drinkers until their son reached about age six. Then, they noticed that he was getting quite wise to the drinking scene. When they'd go out to eat, he would take the initiative and order a beer for Dad and a sherry for Mom.

Some parents might regard such behavior as cute, but this couple immediately began to worry that they were conveying the wrong message to their boy. As a result, they decided to stop drinking altogether as a better example to him.

In addition, the father explained to the child some of the things that were bad about alcohol. He went into some detail about the dangers of drinking and driving, and the various diseases that could result from excessive alcohol use, such as cirrhosis of the liver.

The boy seemed to get the point, and he came away with an education about alcohol that seems to have put him in a position to be safer and to be able to make more intelligent decisions later in life. At this point, eight years after this parent-child discussion took place, the boy has shown no inclination to get involved with alcohol. And I would predict that if this young fellow ever does drink, he'll do so wisely.

Danger Signal #2: Secrecy.

When various pundits talk about parent-child relationships, an overused term is *good communication*. These words reflect an extremely important set of underlying principles. But too often, the catchwords *good communication* are bandied about without any real understanding of their content.

The best word I can think of to describe good communication is *openness*. The child must be willing and able to express his deepest feelings and concerns to the parent; and the parent must be available and discerning in listening and responding to the child.

Conversely, when communications aren't right between parent and child, their relationship tends to be characterized by varying degrees of *secrecy*. For example, in many, many cases that I've encountered of drug use by young people, the parents didn't know what was going on until the substance abuse was well advanced.

One fourteen-year-old girl kept retreating to her room and locking her door. The parents assumed that she was just in one of those stages of development where she required a lot of privacy.

But still, something didn't seem quite right to the mother. For one thing, her daughter seemed exceptionally sullen and uncommunicative around the house. Also, the girl was snappish when the mother knocked on her door or tried to call her to meals or other family gatherings.

Then, when the mother walked in unexpectedly on the daughter in her room one evening, the girl made a motion to cover up something on her dressing table. This action aroused the parents' suspicions, so they conducted a search of the daughter's room one day while she was out and they discovered a cache of cocaine and a collection of pills.

"How could this happen?" the mother wailed to a counselor who had been called in to help with the situation.

The problem arose as a result of a complex set of factors that centered on the girl's feeling that she had been too restricted by her parents. She had developed a deep need to rebel, and using drugs was one way of doing it.

The important thing for us in this illustration is not so much the cause of her rebellion as the significance of the *signal* the daughter was putting out: that is, the unusual degree of secrecy she was displaying. By finally understanding that signal for what it was, the parents were able to step in and take countermeasures designed to put the girl's life back on a better track.

The same kind of secrecy may occur when youngsters are trying to cover up other activities, such as sexual involvement, alcohol use, or smoking. They know they shouldn't be doing what they're doing; they know without a doubt that their parents will disapprove. So they try to hide.

Certainly, it is important to recognize that all children need some privacy, some secret places, thoughts, and activities that only they, by themselves or in the company of certain trusted peers, know about. And the older a child gets, the more "space" and privacy he needs. Consequently, it's necessary for parents to be able to distinguish between a natural, healthy need for privacy and the kind of secrecy that's a danger signal of risky or dangerous behavior.

Keep a few key questions in mind as you're trying to distinguish between your child's normal need for privacy and the secrecy that may be a danger signal.

▶ Has the secrecy occurred abruptly or gradually?

Any abrupt changes in a child's behavior, including a tendency to be more secretive, may indicate that something unhealthy is going on.

▶ Does the secrecy seem to reflect a normal need for privacy, or do you sense something unusual is involved?

I always tell parents it's important for them to trust their instincts. Generally speaking, a mother or father knows a child's typical behavior patterns better than anyone else. So if something *seems* strange, check it out.

▶ Have you been unsuccessful in trying to remain your child's close friend or "pal"?

You may find your youngster rejecting your attempts to retain a previous level of closeness. If you've been close in the past, you may sense a separation or distancing taking place; the child may not want to confide as much in you.

Many times, of course, these tendencies are quite normal. In general, a parent shouldn't expect to be simply a "pal" or "one of the guys" with a son or daughter. To be sure, the parent and the child should be friendly, and that *may* involve an unusual degree of sharing with each other. But then again, the child will probably not want to share everything. Every youngster has to be allowed some privacy and personal space to develop into an independent person.

Also, if a parent gets too close, or becomes too much of a "pal," the necessary authority and leadership he must exercise may be compromised. Therefore, expect to be your child's parent, not a peer, because a parent is what she wants you to be. After all, a child isn't going to obey a peer, no matter how deep the friendship runs. But she should obey a parent.

▶ Do a hard, cold evaluation of your communications with your child over the past couple of days. Do you feel that, on balance, you've been too judgmental, preachy, or negative?

If your answer is yes, you could be pushing your child toward resistance or rebellion, tendencies that can be reflected in unhealthy secrecy. I always suggest to parents that they do periodic evaluations of their own conduct and communications with their children. Mentally, you might put your comments to your child on a scale, and if the negatives outweigh the positives, start focusing more on praise and upbeat interactions.

To address communication issues, some families have a family conference or meeting at the same time every week. During this meeting, each person is permitted to state what he or she thought were good and bad interactions, and to provide suggestions on how to improve things.

▶ Do *you* tend to pick the time and place for intimate conversations rather than allow your child to do so?

I'm reminded of one father who told me, "I can't seem to pry any information out of my daughter about her friends, school experiences, anything!"

His daughter, who was eight years old, tended to clam up when the father wanted to talk, and that was usually immediately after he arrived from work or sat down at the dinner table. As it happened, at those times the girl was usually completely involved in her own play or thoughts and didn't want to open up on a deep level to anyone, including her dad.

On the other hand, she *was* ready to talk when she cuddled up for a bedtime story or when she was in bed after saying her prayers. At those moments, however, the mother was with her. Dad was either too tired to interact or too deeply involved in reading the newspaper or watching TV.

"You've got to let *her* pick the times to open up," I told him. "After all, *you* don't spill your innermost thoughts at someone else's bidding. You do it when you're good and ready, and that's exactly what you have to expect from her!"

So when your child says, "I've got to talk to you," you should never say, "I don't have time now." Nor should you respond, "How about later this afternoon" or "tomorrow." Too often, "later" and "tomorrow" never come. Even if they do, the door to the child's mind and emotions, which may have opened wide for you at that special moment, may close, and you'll miss being admitted to those inner recesses where you can exercise important influence over his future.

To put it in even more simplistic terms, children are human beings, just like adults. But parents often operate as though their youngsters had just arrived from outer space. Believe me, there's nothing that mysterious about child development. Boys and girls have the same basic emotions and needs as their parents, including a natural desire for intimacy and a desire for privacy. But when they're ready to be intimate, we have to be ready to respond. And when they want to be private—and that desire for privacy doesn't signal a dangerous secrecy—we have to give them the space they need.

A key difference between adults and children is that the need to be separate, private, and independent develops over a period of years, as the child grows and becomes more of a separate entity from the parent. At whatever stage the child is in this growth process, his or her feelings and needs must be respected and responded to sensitively and individually. Otherwise, good communication can never develop, and the wrong kind of secrecy is likely to emerge.

Danger Signal #3: A child who is alone too much or too loosely supervised at a relatively young age.

This danger signal of excessive freedom is hard to quantify because some children do quite well when they're alone for long periods of time. Others, in contrast, may get into mischief or threatening situations when they're by themselves for only a few minutes.

In part, this issue is age-related. The older the child, the more he should be able to operate effectively on his own. But still, there's a wide variation in how children of the exact same age can handle their freedom.

One prevalent example of this "being-alone freedom" is what has come to be known as the "latchkey child." According to some estimates, there may be five million or more latchkey kids in the United States. These are defined as children who are left alone to take care of themselves without adult supervision at some time during the day. In many cases, these children are expected to enter empty homes or apartments after school and wait there for their parents or another adult caretaker to arrive.

One nine-year-old who was expected to fend for himself for about two hours after he arrived home from school became unusually fearful. He was constantly worried that his mother, a single parent, would die; that someone would break into his apartment and harm him; or that his mother would come home very late or not at all that day.

As we questioned the boy, it became evident that one of the sources of his fears was the television set. To occupy himself while he was alone, he flicked around on the channels and frequently settled on one of the local news programs, which focused on crime news. When he heard and saw how many people were getting killed, maimed, and robbed around the city, he began to wonder, "Why couldn't that happen to me or my mom?"

Clearly, this boy had been given too much responsibility—and too much freedom—at too young an age. Granted, he was mature beyond his years. But still, he needed an adult around to give him some assurance and support. It wasn't necessary for him to have someone hovering over him every moment, but at that age, he did need some older, loving presence in the background, ready to respond in case of need.

Understand, though, that I'm not suggesting that children this age should never be alone. Actually, it's often quite helpful for a child's growth and development to have the parent leave the youngster by himself for short periods. This sort of approach will enhance feelings of independence in many youngsters and will promote a healthy process of maturing.

But parents must evaluate the special situation and needs of their child and respond accordingly. Some children at age eight or nine shouldn't be left alone because they're naturally fearful, and the solitude aggravates their fears. On the other hand, *most* children of this age that I encounter can be left alone in the house for fifteen minutes or a half-hour. When you leave them alone, you must give them precise information about where you are and how you may be reached. Also, you should give an estimate of when you will return; if a delay occurs, call to explain when you will return. Among other things, the experience gives them a sense of being more mature and grown up.

In the last analysis, then, your final goal as a parent of a growing child is clear. You want to find that happy medium between the destructive latchkey situation and a more constructive loosening of parental control.

Danger Signal #4: A lack of supervision of homework.

Another issue that may highlight the condition of having too much freedom relates to homework. In many schools, teachers emphasize that students should be responsible for their own homework. If they don't do it, it's their problem, not their parents'. There's a great deal to be said for this approach. Ultimately, a child has to learn how to listen to instructions at school, follow them in completing an assignment at home, and then take the responsibility for success or failure in the teacher's grading.

But there's another side to this homework issue. I remember a couple of parents who complained, "Fred simply won't do his homework properly. He's never been motivated to read, and he seems incapable of doing well on even the simplest math problems. I think his teachers have completely fallen down on the job!"

In fact, though, Fred's teachers, who taught at a very good public school, had great reputations for nurturing young intellects to great achievement. At first glance, the problem seemed to lie in Fred more than the teachers. But as we traced the difficulties back to their final source, it became evident that Fred's *parents* had to bear more responsibility for Fred's failure than anyone.

Here's the specific history of Fred's problems. From the time he was very young, his parents had taken a complete hands-off attitude toward his homework. They had heard his teachers say, "The responsibility for homework is up to the child, not the parents." And being quite busy professionals, they had heaved a sigh of relief and completely ignored their son, even when he had asked for help.

On a number of occasions in his early elementary years, he had complained, "I can't figure out these instructions" or "This problem is too hard for me" or "I don't feel like reading anything tonight."

When they heard these remarks from their son, the parents had just concluded, "Okay, if he doesn't do his work, that's between him and his teachers. They'll lean on him to improve if he's not working up to par."

Unfortunately, the parents overlooked the fact that Fred's teachers had to supervise thirty or so other children. They just didn't have the time or energy to give one child special attention. As a result, Fred was left to cope with his homework almost entirely on his own. It was only by receiving low grades that he found out when he had missed the mark on a particular assignment.

When Fred finally reached his early high-school years, he was regarded as a relatively poor student with bad study habits. The problem wasn't that he was by nature unintelligent or incompetent. He had just never been taught or guided in the right academic direction when he was young; he had been given no chance to develop good work habits.

Fred was caught in an unhelpful crossfire. His parents blamed his teachers; and his teachers, when they were confronted with his poor performance, blamed Fred and the parents.

Parents must understand that they do have an important role to play in overseeing their children's homework. No matter what a teacher may tell you or seem to tell you, you must interact constructively with your child on homework assignments. It's important for mothers and fathers to offer encouragement to their child on his academic performance and study habits, or it's likely that the child will fall short of his potential.

Giving freedom to a child to study only when he feels like it isn't freedom at all; it's a form of neglect. To be sure, every successful student has to have some inner motivation and independence in completing his work. Mom or Dad shouldn't do his homework for him, for example. But when a child reaches a real roadblock—when she says, after several attempts, "I just can't figure this out!"—then it's time for parents to lend a hand.

Also, I believe it's important for parents to know what work has been assigned for home and to watch over the process from a background vantage point. Parents of a young child should be especially alert to see that the child has remembered to do everything assigned and also has put in an adequate amount of time to do the best possible job.

Dr. Herbert Walberg of the University of Illinois at Chicago has studied this homework issue thoroughly and has concluded that parental participation is essential for successful academic performance. He says that up to a 50 percent improvement in grades and test scores can be achieved by students whose parents do the following: (1) show a warm interest in the children's work; (2) encourage good reading habits; (3) limit TV watching; (4) engage in conversations about school; and (5) take their children on independent educational outings. This parental approach allows children freedom to develop their academic potential, yet doesn't involve a hands-off kind of neglect.

Danger Signal #5: Plans to send a child to a boarding school or an all-summer camp.

Many times, parents send a child away from home for long stays at a boarding school and/or a summer camp with the rationalization that "this is a wonderful opportunity for Suzy. This will really give her some important new skills and put her at a major advantage in the future."

But if parents look deep inside themselves, they may find that the *real* reason they want to send their child to these places is that they want someone else to take care of the child. They just want to be free of the responsibility.

Again, though, I don't want to be doctrinaire or legalistic about this. Obviously, some children do quite well in a boarding school environment. Even more children, especially those who are in their teen years or older, thrive at long summer camps where they can participate in sports and outdoor activities.

Finding out where you and your child stand on this issue requires considerable soul-searching and a balancing of several significant factors. Some of these factors are indicated by the following questions, which I often put to parents in this position.

▶ Do you feel you've given your child most of the basic instruction you can on the values you hold dear?

Remember, if you send your child away during most of the school year, or even all summer, you'll be relinquishing much of this influence to others. Perhaps your youngster is already fairly mature, in the sense that he or she has absorbed most of the principles of morality and spirituality that you can provide. But the situation is different if you feel your son or daughter is *not* mature. You may know that you still have some basic lessons to impart or that your child hasn't completely learned what you've been teaching. In such circumstances, your youngster may be better off spending more time around home.

▶ Is your child still of elementary school age—about twelve years old or younger?

If so, I personally wouldn't consider boarding school. I'm generally opposed to boarding schools, except in unique situations. Even a relatively mature child who is in the ninth grade, or about fourteen years old, isn't always ready to move away from home and be placed under the influence of even the most responsible teachers and headmasters. The parents have major roles to play in these formative teen years, and I don't think they should abdicate their responsibility.

In the early elementary school years, a short stay—say, for a couple of weeks—in a sleep-away camp may be an exciting and constructive experience for some children. But parents must not push the issue. If your son or daughter expresses a strong desire to attend such a camp, that's a good sign that the time is right. But if the child is quite hesitant or fearful, it's best to wait.

Older children—say, those ten years old or older—can certainly benefit from longer stays away from home, including longer summer camps. But again, you should be sensitive to the individual child's needs and interests.

The most important need any child has at any age is *you!* If you cause your child to be on her own too much, apart from your guidance at too young an age, that's not freedom to grow. Such independence can backfire and cause tremendous insecurities, which may lead to underachievement and even serious emotional problems and physical disorders.

An account by Michael Norman, a columnist for the *New York*

Times, provides poignant reminiscences of the problems with leaving home at a too-young age. Norman says, "I encountered the mystery of men and loneliness" at a boarding school where his parents put him at the tender age of ten.

In his 1988 essay entitled "The Road To Self-Reliance," he writes,

> The lesson of boarding school was the lesson of separation, perhaps the fundamental lesson of manhood: through codes and rituals, men are taught to remove themselves and live a step apart. There is no reaching across that space—no handhold for . . . the mothers who left them behind.

Before the boarding school experience, he recalls,

> I do not think I knew what loneliness was. . . . I can easily summon to the surface the deep ache of that first night in my room as I looked out between the mullions into the darkness at the car lights creeping across the bridge. Nothing dulled that ache, not puppets brought from home and held close in bed, not the nurse with the soft hands in the infirmary, not even the infrequent notes from my mother on her scented letterhead.

Norman's reminiscences highlight some of the deepest fears I harbor for children who attend boarding schools or long summer camps for the wrong reasons.

Danger Signal #6: A tendency to make "appointments" with your child or otherwise engage in excessively formal interactions.

Do you ever find that you have to make an "appointment" with your child to be able to spend any time with him? Or do you sense that your relationship with your youngster is becoming too formal or unspontaneous in other ways?

A chronic condition that emerges in many busy families these days is overscheduling. In fact, many families don't even have all members together for at least one meal every day. Ironically, the very act of setting up too many things for parent *or* child to do can cause a youngster to be too free or uninvolved with parents. This is precisely the type of freedom from parental influence that can lead to serious problems.

Here, by the way, I'm not only talking about doing too many things or becoming too busy with a surfeit of activities. Even more important, I'm referring to the tendency to set up deadlines and activities on such split-second timing that there's no room for relaxed, spontaneous interactions between parents and children.

There should always be room for spontaneity, even when a child's jokes, antics, or desire to talk about some special event or concern throws other scheduled activities off their pace. Yet more than a few families I know have stifled this freewheeling kind of interaction.

In one situation, both the mother and the father set aside a few minutes to be with their three children each evening. The parents held down demanding jobs, which prevented them from getting home until about 7:00 P.M. or even later on typical days.

The children, who ranged in age from three to nine, were all supposed to be in bed by 9:00 P.M. So by the time the parents had arrived home, changed into some comfortable clothes, said a few words to each other, and then put dinner on the table, it was nearly 8:00 P.M. That left only about an hour for eating and spending a short period with each child—hardly enough time for relaxed conversation.

Because of the time squeeze the parents felt with their schedule, they tended to demand a certain degree of regimentation from the children. When one or more of the youngsters balked at the pressure, the parents resorted to negative forms of discipline, such as verbal reprimands or sending a child to his or her room. All in all, most evenings in this home weren't very pleasant.

In similar family situations, where the children are in their teenage years, silence, stiff conversations, and even a degree of wariness may characterize parent-child interactions. The youngsters seem to understand that their parents don't have that much time for them. Furthermore, they sense that if they try to vary the schedule that has been set up, they'll run into parental opposition and maybe punishment. So they just decide to back off and look elsewhere for intimate, relaxed relationships.

In one such family, a boy had been "programmed" from an early age to participate in many after-school activities. Also, he was allotted very little time just to talk and cuddle with Mom or Dad. Consequently, this boy began to develop very dependent attachments to other children and even to their parents. Anyone who would give him some time and take notice of him could get his attention. In his teens, this boy began to "hang out" with friends after school instead of paying attention to his homework. He dropped all extracurricular activities because, as he said, "I can't stand them! I don't know why, but I just can't bear the thought of being required to attend another music class or tennis lesson."

It became obvious that he was reacting to the overregimentation he had experienced when he was younger. Even more important, he was looking for personal involvements and relationships that had been denied him earlier. "Hanging out" seemed to provide some of the interactions that he had lacked.

Unfortunately, this boy was so peer-oriented that he more or less went along with the crowd. He was petrified at the idea that his new friends might reject him, so he took drugs when they did or engaged in sex to boast and get their approval.

Finally, he had to be treated for herpes and for drug abuse, and he entered psychotherapy. In the course of these treatments, the boy and his parents came to realize that their pattern of overscheduling had backfired.

"You shouldn't keep trying to get your child to participate in 'constructive' activities at school or elsewhere, as you did when he was quite young," they were told. "That obviously didn't work. What he needs is not a lot of busyness and appointments to fill up his time each day. Rather, what he needs is *love,* and that should come from *you,* his mother and father."

I'm happy to report that in this case, the boy's life was actually able to be turned around. Both his mother and his father took the advice to heart and began to treat him as a special person who was just as important as their work or other activities. They spent much more time with him, and for the first time, parents and son actually got to know one another.

Certainly, there were disagreements and misunderstandings, as there are in any relationship. But all concerned really wanted to make their family work. Gradually, they began to recoup the family love and satisfaction they had lost years earlier.

But understand this: I'm *not* citing this example to suggest that it's all right to wait until your child gets older to eliminate "appointments," formal interactions, and overscheduling. Rather, it's best to act when your child is young—when negative patterns and habits haven't yet become deeply ingrained in your relationship.

On the other hand, I *do* want to inject a note of positive possibility here. Even if your child is relatively old, all is not lost! You can still make a difference if you take decisive action to change the unproductive situation in which you find yourselves.

Danger Signal #7: A child's tendency to get involved in accidents or risky situations.

One set of parents brought their young daughter and son to see me seven or eight times one year, and in every case, the problem was an injury caused by an accident. I don't worry about one or two accidents because active children do bang themselves around as they're growing up. But in this case, I found myself dealing with a mild concussion, a broken wrist, and a cut on the lower leg of one child, just to mention the serious injuries.

In such cases, physicians always want to check out the possibility of child abuse. But that wasn't the situation here. What I discovered after a thorough investigation was that the children, who were three and five years old, had been allowed to roam at will around the couple's country house on weekends and during the summer. There were many precarious ditches, bramble bushes, old walls, and abandoned structures on the property—tantalizing but quite dangerous for children who hadn't developed a mature sense of judgment about what was simply fun and what was a physical threat. If any description could be used for the situation, it would be parental neglect.

When I suggested that these parents should supervise their youngsters more closely, the father at first gave me an argument: "I want them to be risk takers! They have to learn by trial and error what they can do and what they can't do. If I don't give them some freedom and encourage them to step out, they'll be too timid to achieve in life."

"They may not be alive at all if you're not careful," I said. I pointed out that the family was quite lucky that the last injury—a concussion that had occurred to the boy when he had fallen after a rotten tree limb had broken under his weight—hadn't been more serious. After a more complete discussion with me, the parents agreed the problems represented neglect out of misdirected good intentions. We made plans to set reasonable boundaries for their children.

Certainly, children should not be overprotected as they're growing up. They have to try their wings and extend themselves as they test developing skills. At the same time, however, if parents allow young children free rein in dangerous or risky situations, the disastrous results of a risk may well outweigh the potential rewards.

Still, I don't want to seem overly restrictive. Even in large cities, for instance, eight- or nine-year-old children *may* be able to play without direct adult supervision—and without bad results—for an hour or more with other youngsters in neighborhood playgrounds. I know of many cases where this sort of thing occurs, with absolutely no injuries or accidents. In general, this loosening of restrictions is part of the process of becoming more independent and self-confident and of separating from parental protection and supervision.

But parents must exercise discretion in these situations. An eight-year-old child who is inclined to disobey or "forget" parental rules and instructions may not be ready for this sort of independence. Also, if the playgrounds in your area are frequented by older children you don't know, or who seem rough or dangerous, you obviously won't want to expose your child to this experience.

Back yard facilities, such as jungle gyms and swimming pools, can also be two-edged swords in the exercise of childhood freedom. They may at first *seem* safe, primarily because they are familiar, and there's no doubt that the opportunity for vigorous exercise is a wonderful advantage for children whose parents can afford such benefits.

But these at-home play areas can also harbor major hazards for children. One study published by the *Journal of the American Medical Association* in 1988 identified private swimming pools as a growing danger for youngsters. In Los Angeles County, 45 percent of drowning deaths involve private pools, according to Dr. Patrick O'Carroll of the National Center for Disease Control.

"Drowning has become an accident of affluence," Dr. James Orlowski of the Cleveland Clinic Foundation reported.

Toddlers especially were shown to be at risk in the Los Angeles studies; nine in ten drownings involving children of this age group occurred in private pools.

Danger Signal #8: Sexual involvement.

One of the most difficult issues facing modern parents is how to handle a child's emerging sexuality. It may seem to have been much easier in the past, when moral standards were clearer and stricter rules about relationships were more generally accepted. But there have always been worries and challenges about teenage sex that have caused parents particular problems.

Too often—and this was especially true twenty-five or more years ago—parents have just avoided the issue. With sex, as in no other area, moms and dads have often just taken a silent, detached position. At most, the typical parents have been inclined to tell their child something about the "facts of life," and then they've backed away and let the youngster fend for herself.

In a sense, it becomes a "dance of mystery." The parents wonder, "Are they or aren't they having sex? But I'd better not broach the subject because something unpleasant may happen if I ask them about it!"

The youngsters think, "They can't talk to us effectively about sex because they're too embarrassed or traditional or old-fashioned. So there's no point in our bringing the topic up."

As a result, the entire parent-child interaction becomes halting and uncertain, rather than free and constructive. In many such cases, sexual involvement is a danger signal of too much freedom because parents have relinquished any voice of authority about their children's emerging sex lives. Children are allowed to operate on their own in this area, and frequently, they get into big trouble before they even realize what is happening to them.

I'm *not* suggesting that sex is somehow bad or that those who are moving into their teens shouldn't learn how to relate to the opposite sex. Rather, I just want to highlight the fact that even though you may try to ignore the reality of the situation, the teen's sex drive and sexual curiosity will still be there.

Furthermore, without your help and guidance, your child will likely be rocked violently about in this area without a moral anchor or the knowledge and skills necessary to navigate this treacherous sexual sea. The result may be far more uncomfortable and embarrassing than if you had just met the issue head-on when your child was much younger.

One sixteen-year-old boy had a rash in the groin area. The rash was what doctors would call "nonspecific." That is, the precise nature or cause of the problem wasn't clear on an initial examination; so further tests were required to determine the source of the problem.

As he and I talked, it became obvious that the boy thought the rash might have been sexually transmitted. But when I questioned him about his sexual activities further, he clammed up.

Despite his denials, I forged ahead because I felt we were on an important track: "You know, there are times when a rash or sores may appear in the genital area if you have sex unprotected, without a condom."

"Oh, no, that couldn't be my problem because I haven't had sex," he protested again.

"Of course, it's possible if you've worn a bathing suit a lot recently, and you were in the sand, a rash could have occurred as a result of irritation," I said. Then I continued to talk in more general terms about his health, though coming back periodically to sex in as natural a way as I could.

Finally, the boy began to feel more comfortable with me. He said, "Well, I've got to tell you the truth. You see, I always wanted to have sex with this one girl, but she wouldn't let me. And I respected that. But then, I met this other girl . . ."

One thing led to another, he said, and he did have sex several times with the second girl. But he also began to feel guilty about this relationship because the first girl was the one he really cared about. It became evident as he talked that, somehow, he felt he was being punished with the rash because he had engaged in sex with the second girl. To make things even more complicated, he had also had sexual intercourse with a *third* girl in the past month while he was on a vacation to Florida.

Where were his parents during this time? They were in the distant background, supplying him with money to take these trips and go out on expensive dates. But they weren't giving him what he really needed: a willing ear and authoritative advice about his increasingly uncontrolled sexual expression. That role had fallen to me, and I did as well as I could under the circumstances.

I performed a series of tests on him and finally determined that his rash was *not* sexually induced. The boy was quite relieved by this news, but it was evident that he still felt uncomfortable and unhappy with himself and his behavior.

As we talked, by the way, I didn't simply dismiss his feelings of discomfort and guilt. Instead, I tried to show him that his uncomfortable sense about himself and his behavior was well-founded. He *had* been acting irresponsibly, both toward himself and toward the young women in his life—for several reasons.

First of all, I told him, if he continued to express his sexual urges as he had been doing, he was almost certain to get a sexually transmitted disease. And that disease might very well be one of the kinds for which there is currently no known cure.

Second, if he engaged in multiple sexual relationships and contracted a disease, he was likely to pass that disease on to his partners, including the girl he really loved. "If you feel guilty now, think what you'll feel like after doing that!" I said.

Finally, I brought the matter back to the basic question of morality. "What do you think is right in this situation? And what do you think is wrong?" I asked. You'll note that I *didn't* hit him over the head with a judgmental, this–is–evil accusation. Rather, I gave him an opportunity to reveal and affirm his own principles and values.

As I had expected, he replied: "I think I shouldn't play around with these girls. I think that's wrong."

It was easy for me to affirm that conclusion, and I told him that I wanted him to feel free to check with me any time he had problems or questions in this area. "Don't wait until something goes wrong before you see me, either!" I said. "It's often a lot easier for a doctor to help prevent a problem *before* it occurs than it is to find a cure afterward."

I heard from this boy once or twice after this meeting, and I have every reason to believe that he changed his sexual behavior. But of course, I'm not his parent, and I don't have the opportunity to be in constant, close touch with him. On the other hand, for a few brief moments, I had the privilege of stepping into the position of a parent for him. I only wish that his real parents could have assumed that role on an ongoing basis, but from what I could tell, they never did.

The sexual signals during adolescence are among the most difficult for parents to deal with. One reason is that the whole subject
sometimes seems too private and embarrassing to discuss. We can
talk freely, at least in abstract terms, with our peers about sex. But
when it comes to delving into this topic with our children, there are
all sorts of social and emotional roadblocks.

The challenge for those of us who are parents is to do all we can
to shape our children's sexual attitudes and behaviors. Without such
help from us, our children, once again, will be in a situation where
they have too much freedom for their level of experience and matu-
rity.

Danger Signal #9: Lack of household responsibilities.

By far, in the majority of middle- and upper-middle-class families I've dealt with, the children have few, if any, household duties
assigned to them. Some parents seem to feel that if they always wait
on their children, they provide the children with more free time.
Others prefer to do the jobs quickly rather than wait for their children's slower, less efficient cleanup to proceed.

Yet I feel this freedom from work around the home encourages
a cavalier or even neglectful attitude toward fundamental responsibilities. Take the issue of keeping toys put away or the children's
room and play areas neat.

One father of a six-year-old boy complained to me, "I can't
seem to get Allen to understand that he has to learn to take care of his
things. His mother and I tell him that he must pick up his toys and
put them on a proper shelf when he has finished playing with them.
But he usually forgets. Or if he remembers, he resists the idea of
performing any duties that aren't 'fun.'

"So I've tried punishing him—taking away TV when he doesn't
do his jobs. That works for a while, but when I fail to impose the
punishment, he reverts to his same old sloppiness. He's a terrible
example for his little sister, who is already showing signs of the same
kind of behavior. I'm worried that both our kids are going to be
completely irresponsible slobs when they grow up!"

This father's experience was typical of that of many parents. He
and his wife had bought literally hundreds of toys for Allen and his
younger sister. The children often liked to play with a variety of dif-

ferent toys at one sitting. Consequently, by the time they "set up" their play area for their fantasy games, the entire floor would be covered. But then, when they finished, it was frequently up to the parents to put things back in order.

I told this father that he should keep several points in mind in dealing with this problem. First of all, he was on the right track in trying to instill in his children a sense of responsibility for personal possessions and household tasks. Without this responsibility, there would be too much of the wrong kind of freedom in their lives—a freedom that could easily lead to *ir*responsibility and excessive disorder as adults.

At the same time, however, he needed to set his sights a little lower about what children are able to do at a young age. In nursery schools, many boys and girls who are barely beyond the toddler stage can be taught to pick up their toys and place them precisely on a designated shelf. But that doesn't always work quite so smoothly at home.

In part, the reason for this difference between school and home is that teachers are usually placed in a more authoritarian role than parents. They are dealing with many children, and a stern word from teacher, along with the pressure of peer approval, causes most children to do what they're told.

Parents, on the other hand, tend to have more of a one-to-one relationship with their children and relate to them in looser, less structured settings. There's more room to argue or resist what Mom or Dad says. As a result, most children don't respond quite as obediently at home as they do at school.

Also, an emotional letdown always occurs when the child leaves the higher pressured school environment and enters the warmer, more lenient envelope of home. Frequently, that letdown is expressed in the opposite behavior from what the child is accustomed to at school, including more resistance to authority and increased messiness.

So I told this father not to expect his children to perform with military precision in picking up their toys. If they did turn out to be extremely neat, that would be a bonus. But perhaps it should be acceptable for them to pick up only half their toys or to push them in a less-than-perfect pile in one corner of the room.

Third, I pointed out that the process of developing orderliness in one's life is a gradual thing, with many stops and starts. Further, not all children are naturally neat, whereas others are. "So don't expect your youngsters to become perfectly neat overnight," I cautioned.

For example, the children might first learn to pile their toys in one corner of the room. Then, they might later learn to sort their toys into separate boxes or onto shelves.

One way to motivate them in this direction would be to leave the toys in the original pile. Then, when one of the children wanted a particular toy, he would inevitably ask, "Mom (or Dad), where is my . . . ?"

Of course, Mom or Dad wouldn't know any more about where that toy was than the child. After all, the child created the pile! So the parent might respond, "You're the one who put the toys in that pile. You'll have to find it."

After a couple of experiences wading through dozens of toys to find the desired item, a child will often learn the merits of being neater and more orderly.

Finally, I've found it's quite helpful to bring the child into the decision-making process of establishing responsibilities and duties around the home. A family meeting might be called, and the issues outlined: "Toys are scattered around the house too much. What do you suggest we do about this?"

With this approach, the child will often assign *himself* certain tasks and will be far more likely to carry them out. In such a discussion, it may be helpful to make certain rewards or privileges depend on the performance of the assigned duties, again, with the child's agreement.

For example, a youngster may agree to pick up his toys and otherwise clean up his room in return for the privilege of watching television for a set period of time on Saturday morning. If he fails to do his cleanup duties one day, he'll fail to qualify for the full privilege. If he doesn't do his job for two days, he'll qualify for even less TV time—and so forth.

When the child participates in the decision-making process, the likelihood increases considerably that he'll become a more responsible member of the family. With that sense of responsibility comes a *genuine* kind of freedom—a freedom to be a well-regarded and productive member of whatever community in which he finds himself.

Danger Signal #10: A failure to influence your child's choice of friends.

When children are young, parents may exercise some degree of control over their playmates. But what are the standards for selecting a child's friends at an early age? In talking with parents, I often find that a major consideration is how well they get along with other caretakers or parents.

On one level, of course, if you are in the habit of setting up play dates for your child, you'll probably be sensitive to whether or not your child likes the other child. But in a surprising number of cases, if a parent likes another parent, he or she will override a child's protest: "Oh, you'll like to play with so-and-so when you get over there."

The compatibility of nonparental caretakers may be another controlling factor. Assume for a moment that a baby sitter is involved in taking care of the child. Almost inevitably, I find that unless directed otherwise, the sitter will choose to have a child play in a location where there's another baby sitter the first sitter likes.

Obviously, this attitude has everything backward. Caretaker compatibility should *not* be the controlling consideration; the compatibility of the children should be. In many cases, however, the reverse becomes the rule of thumb. So it may be necessary to make a *conscious decision* to push aside the issue of how well baby sitters get along and focus on the compatibility of the children.

As boys and girls get older, they tend to exercise more authority in choosing their friends. But parents should still try to exert influence for as long as they possibly can over these relationships. Simply asking about a friendship helps the child focus on the relationship and on why it's so important to the youngster. I advise parents with older children to keep a few points in mind.

Don't become an interrogator.

Parents tell me frequently, "I keep asking her, who are your friends? Who are you hanging out with? But I can't get anything out of her."

I suggest that such parents put themselves in the child's position. How would *they* like to be questioned this way? No older child or adult wants to be put on the spot about activities and friendships. So be more subtle and indirect. Engage in a friendly conversation with your child, and work your way around to the friendship situation. This way, you're much more likely to find out what you need to know and to be in a position to help out.

Don't order your child to stop being friends with someone.

That's the best way to ensure that the friendship will continue. I've met very few well-adjusted children who respond well to statements like, "You've *got* to do this or that!" That's preaching, not intimate, one-to-one discussion. Yet you need the intimacy if you hope to influence your youngster's friendships.

Show your child what true friendship involves.

The best way to get this point across is through "show and tell." That is, establish your own meaningful friendships, and then point out the strong points to your youngster.

Another constructive way to get this message across is to select a relaxed, unthreatening time to engage in a friendly conversation with your child. Then, steer the talk around to the meaning of friendship. Ask your child to tell you why she thinks she has a certain friend; then you give your version of why the friendship exists.

You also might start out something like this: "You know, we haven't talked much about this, but let me pass on something to you for what it's worth. Over the years, I've found my friendships to be one of the most important parts of my life. I've made some mistakes along the way, but I've also discovered some important principles that I try to follow."

Then, illustrate the mistakes and the principles through concrete examples. Finally, you might ask, "Have you had any thoughts or experiences like this?" Since you've already opened up, your child will be more likely to open up.

Help your child avoid difficult or dangerous situations with friends.

Young people today face tremendous stresses when they find themselves in social situations they can't handle. Yet with a little parental guidance and help, they could avoid many of these pressures.

Some parents I know allowed their twelve-year-old daughter to get trapped in encounters where great pressure was placed on her to engage in sex. She was permitted to be at events that weren't adequately chaperoned. Several of her best friends had already had some level of sexual activity, but this girl wasn't even ready for hand-holding. Yet she began to feel that if she didn't give in, at least for some kissing, she would be excluded from her peer group.

Finally, this girl went to her mother for advice, and Mom promptly put the situation in perspective. "Your instincts are exactly right," the mother said, reassuringly. "And those other kids are heading for trouble."

Then, the mother summarized some potential dangers: sexually transmitted diseases, an unwanted pregnancy, and the violation of the daughter's personal moral code. Throughout the discussion, the mother was firm and authoritative, but not heavy-handed or judgmental. She knew that ultimately, her daughter would have to make her own decisions because she wasn't constantly under the mother's watchful eye.

The final result was comforting to both mother and daughter. The girl came away from the session with the confirmation that her natural resistance to having sex at this time in her life was right. And she also felt reassured that her mother cared for her and supported her.

Parents also need to know as much as possible about the families and family habits of children's friends. Two pertinent examples come to mind.

In one case, a nine-year-old boy went to a friend's home for a sleep-over. Only later did the parents of the visiting boy learn that the other family allowed their son to stay up late and watch R-rated movies on television. As a result, the parents of the visiting boy resolved that sleep-over dates were not going to be permitted with this particular friend. Also, they determined to question the parents of their son's friends more closely about activities planned for their son before a visit.

In another situation, a fourteen-year-old boy went to a swimming party at the home of a young friend. A number of adults who were present were doing some heavy drinking. To make matters worse, the young teenagers were allowed to have a few drinks.

These parents concluded that the situation wasn't appropriate for their son, and they told him he couldn't visit that friend under those circumstances again. As for the boy, he had been feeling extremely uncomfortable at the gathering, and he was rather relieved to hear his parents' plan.

Adolescence is a very tough time for children because they are in transition between childhood and adulthood. They often don't know where they fit in with certain groups, and they frequently run into situations that challenge their values or cause moral confusion. Physical changes are also occurring, and that can be cause for embarrassment in certain circumstances.

So it's important for parents to listen closely for expressions of discomfort or quandary and be ready to respond lovingly and constructively. This type of child-rearing is just as important for teens as for young children. A parent who is able to guide a child through friendships and situations during this difficult period can make life *much* easier for the youngster. On the other hand, failing to intervene in helping a child choose his friends and social activities may actually serve to infringe on the child's freedom to interact constructively with others.

Danger Signal #11: Fuzzy values.

Another sign that a child may be involved in a situation with destructive freedom is a lack of clear rules of morality and conduct around the home. Parent-teacher meetings at many schools reflect this concern. At one such gathering, an anguished mother said to a teacher, "My daughter [an eight-year-old] is constantly using profane language around the house. What can I do about it?"

Any mother with a clear sense of her own set of values should have already had an answer for this question. For example, Mom might just instruct the child that bad language is morally wrong and unacceptable, and she's not to engage in it. Such an admonition should have considerable effect on an eight-year-old—at least so long as the parents or other children don't act as poor role models for the child. Obviously, a mother who swears isn't going to be able to convince a child of any age that clean language is the best approach.

Many parents have found the following guidelines to be helpful in promoting clear-cut values.

Don't be afraid to establish basic rules for right and wrong.

So many parents I encounter feel they have to give every side of a moral question, even to a four-year-old. But that's not necessary! If a question about the rightness or wrongness of a certain behavior arises, just say something like this: "The *right* thing to do here is. . ."; "God teaches us that we should respect others"; "We don't use that kind of language"; or "The right thing to do is to tell the truth, not to lie."

Intelligent children will inevitably raise questions about moral rules, especially as they get older. But if you can teach them while they're quite young to accept certain types of language or action, and to reject others, it's likely that these early lessons will carry over to later life.

Emphasize the positive more than the negative.

Sometimes it's necessary to stress that something is wrong. But whenever possible, cast the lesson in positive terms. You might tell your child, "It's best to play with *every* child who wants to play on the playground instead of telling someone you don't want him around."

Also, tell your child to find ways to enjoy everyone. Look for the good traits and play to them.

Expect your child to test the limits of the rules.

The old adage, "rules are made to be broken," was made to order for the modern-day child. If you tell your youngster not to do something, the chances are that at some point, she will do it. When that happens, you have to be ready to reprimand or withdraw privileges. The rules will inevitably be broken, but you ignore these violations at your peril. A disregarded rule is no rule at all. However, rules that are rewarded are easier to maintain than those for which punishment is the result.

Make your personal values a natural part of your family life.

In one family I know, the father reads the Bible to his nine-year-old child every night, a practice they have been following since the boy was in nursery school. During these readings, the father often discusses how the biblical stories and principles apply to everyday life.

For example, he once read the boy the passage where Jesus says, "It is more blessed to give than to receive." Then, father and son launched into a discussion of how they each had felt when they recently served some street people a Thanksgiving dinner at an urban mission.

The son said, quite honestly, that he felt rather uncomfortable because there were so few other children at the mission that day. He and the father discussed how the situation might have been changed to make him feel more comfortable. They decided that the next time they did something like that, they would choose an opportunity to help out children as well as adults.

The key was not what the father and son concluded about that particular situation, but how they applied their values on an ongoing basis in their daily lives. Morality in this family wasn't an abstract affair; it was something that was practiced naturally.

Danger Signal #12: Medical or emotional disorders.

Many times, children who experience too much of the wrong kind of freedom—or too much of some of the other types of excesses I'll be discussing in this book—may exhibit certain medical or emotional disorders. A few of the possible manifestations are noted below.

But you should not use these descriptions to make your own diagnosis. In fact, any of these disorders may arise from problems *other than* having excessive freedom or having too much of the other types of things that I'll be describing later. You should leave it up to your physician to determine the precise source of the medical or emotional difficulty and to describe the appropriate treatment.

Depression

Depression among children is a condition that's been recognized only recently. In the past, adults have often regarded children as little creatures "without a care in the world." Few people took children's symptoms of depression seriously. But in the last decade or so, increasing numbers of medical experts have come to recognize depression as a peculiar, chronic problem among many children.

Typically, a child who is depressed will exhibit symptoms like these: irritability; a tendency to cry often; insomnia; agitation; and an inclination toward low self-esteem and a low sense of self-worth.[1] Also, the depressed child may suffer from regular headaches, loss of appetite, and chronic fatigue.

The cause of depression will vary from child to child, as is the case with adults. Sometimes, the basis of the depression is *genetic;* in other words, there may be an inherited neurobiochemical tendency in the child to become depressed. If this is the case, psychotherapy and a mood-elevating medication may be appropriate. If left untreated, this type of depression may worsen and may result in severe, ongoing unhappiness or even suicide.

Other times, the depression may be *reactive.* That is, something may be going on in the child's life that triggers the symptoms of depression. If that factor is removed, the depression will most likely disappear. Drugs are rarely required in such a case. Instead, the approach to treatment first should consist of recognizing the cause of depression. Then, if the demonstrated cause can't be changed or avoided, the child should be taught more suitable responses to the offending factor.

There's a tendency for many parents to think, "Our child has to have medications to stay under control." Or children may come to believe, "I can't function without my pills." But when certain environmental causes are removed, the depression may lift.

Reactive depression is most likely to be the sort that's involved when a child is experiencing excessive freedom, including a lack of necessary authority and parental control. One eleven-year-old girl had been crying almost every day, both when she was at school and when she arrived home. Also, she frequently made statements like, "I'm no good" or "I can't do anything right."

This girl had a clear case of depression, and during exploratory conversations, the reason became fairly clear. She was a latchkey child who spent several hours a day at home alone during the week. On weekends, a sitter took her to various activities, including music lessons and sports events.

What this girl needed most in her life was a predictable, loving set of authority figures. She had questions about sex, about friendships, about problems with teachers. But there never seemed to be opportunities to talk with her parents, both of whom spent most of their time in their offices or away on business trips. Her father rarely arrived at home before 8:00 P.M., and the girl was an early-to-bed type. She was usually in bed or well on the way by the time Dad got there. The mother was also frequently home at a late hour. And both parents worked on weekends or went to social gatherings where children weren't welcome.

Because of this family situation, the daughter frequently found herself alone, trying to wrestle with questions and issues she couldn't resolve. Finally, she began to give up, and the result was depression, including frequent weepiness and intense, ongoing sadness.

When the parents were made aware of the situation, they responded admirably. In fact, the physician who was treating the girl was quite surprised because many times, ambitious, busy parents like these *seem* concerned, but they can never make time to give their youngster what he or she needs.

In this case, however, the mother began to get home earlier every evening, and she made certain that the same person, carefully selected by the parents and approved by the girl, was there to meet the girl every day when she arrived home from school. Also, both the mother and the father cut back on their social schedule and weekend workload and made more time to be with their daughter.

The result? The depression lifted almost immediately.

Physical disorders

Whenever a child complains to me about abdominal pain, chest pain, headaches, or fatigue, I think of physical causes as well as psychological ones. I do tests and ask questions designed to lead me to the *real* cause for these complaints. Frequently, there is no physical basis for the problem, but there *may* be psychological causes. In these circumstances, the complaint of pain may be quite real, but the source of the difficulty is psychosomatic. That is, psychological stress or anguish gets converted into a physical manifestation.

For example, the family may have moved; a parent's job may have changed; the child may have suffered the loss of a pet; or a close friend of the child may have left town.[2]

Other causes of these psychosomatic complaints may involve the excess of freedom we've been talking about, or any of the other types of excesses we'll be discussing in this book. If a child feels that he or she isn't really loved or cared for—despite many material advantages—that may create uncertainties and stresses, which can emerge in physical complaints.

If you have questions about the doctor's diagnosis, it's perfectly acceptable and advisable to seek a second opinion from another physician. This approach would be especially appropriate before you subject your child to expensive and extensive radiology tests like a barium swallow to examine the upper GI tract, a barium enema to visualize the lower intestines, or an involved neurologic test such as a CAT scan.

In any event, you should work closely with your physician in trying to identify the source of your child's physical complaints. A pain in the stomach may reflect a serious physical problem, like appendicitis, or a less serious one, like constipation. A trained pediatrician will frequently be able to tell after a careful evaluation whether a child's complaints are physically or emotionally based.

Chapter Five

Kids Who Have Too Much Money

More than once, I've heard wealthy business or professional people say, "You can never have too much money!" Some mean that no matter how much you have, it never seems to be enough to cover financial commitments and expenses. Others are referring to the idea that accumulating a lot of money is an entirely acceptable and worthy pursuit in life.

Certainly, I don't have any objections if any person—man, woman, or child—wants to earn as much money as possible. Nor do I take issue with the idea that regardless of one's income or assets, there never seem to be sufficient personal funds to pay for everything. So in some ways, perhaps you really never can have enough money.

On the other hand, there is a way that you *can* have too much money—if you possess it or use it so as to distort more important values and relationships. Furthermore, children, as well as adults, may be susceptible to this trap.

Ten-year-old Don came home and told his parents that a classmate had given him several dollars, *apparently* with no strings attached. When his father questioned him about the reason for the payment, Don replied, "He just gave it to me. I didn't have to do anything for it."

"People don't just give you money for nothing, Don," his father responded. "Your schoolmate must have wanted something. Think about it and see if you can remember anything."

As they talked, Don did recall several "give-backs" that seemed

93

to be associated with the payment. The boy had indicated that he wanted Don to be his friend.

"What's the money for?" Don had asked.

"Nothing—just something between friends," his classmate had said.

After handing over the money, the boy had made several requests of Don later in the day: "Will you tell John I'll be waiting for him outside school today?"; "Would you mind lending me some sheets of notepaper?"; "Do you want to get together to play basketball over the weekend?"

All of these requests, while relatively innocent in themselves, were unusual in that the boy had never asked anything of Don before. Also, the requests came soon after the payment of money, as though the boy assumed that the payment entitled him to something.

Don's father didn't have to explain the connection between the passing of the money and the boy's behavior. It was now quite obvious to Don.

"He wants me to be his go-fer!" Don exclaimed. "He's paying me to do things for him!"

"He also seems to be paying you to be his friend," the father added. "But you know, this boy probably isn't even completely aware of what he's doing."

Like many other children, Don's classmate apparently had been conditioned to focus more on money and material possessions than on relationships and authentic values. From what Don's father knew of the family, it seemed likely that the other boy had been taught through his parents' example that material things were an adequate substitute for human relationships, or at least a means to such relationships.

The resolution of this issue became quite clear as father and son talked. Don found he didn't want money to play a part in his friendships. He saw that accepting a few dollars could put him in the position of owing far more in terms of his time and allegiance. So he determined not to allow money to play any role in his human associations.

In the previous chapters, we considered how various circumstances can lead to destructive freedom in a child's life. Here, we see how another factor, too much money, can actually limit a desirable kind of freedom—the capacity of a young person to choose his friends, associates, and activities. Also, as those schooled in Christian thought and morality will readily see, we appear to have here contemporary evidence for the truth of the biblical admonition, "The love of money is a root of all kinds of evil," (1 Tim. 6:10).

Too much money can also shackle a child in other ways. Take the case of the person who inherits wealth or who knows he or she will receive a lump sum on reaching a certain age. What does this financial safety net do to the ambition and self-esteem of the recipient?

The Curse of Family Wealth

"Too much of any good thing is fatal," says investment expert John Train, head of a firm that specializes in advising rich families.

In evaluating the status of fourteen adult children, who are the fourth generation of a wealthy old New York family, Train notes, "Not one of them holds a conventional job. I think that's terrible."[1]

Several reports have dealt with this condition, which has been called "affluenza." These investigations have revealed several characteristics common among children who are the heirs of family wealth.

A failure to mature emotionally. Being protected or insulated by access to too much money can give a child the impression that he deserves or is somehow naturally entitled to money without having to work for it. Such an attitude, of course, is highly immature. A child may be fortunate enough to have the advantage of family wealth. But he or she should learn to view and use that wealth actively and constructively and not simply rely on it as a womblike protection from the real world.

As a San Francisco consultant to heirs and heiresses, John Levy, has put it: "There's a lack of reality because there's no price to pay. They can go out and do something stupid or wrong and be bailed out. It's almost like being in a movie."[2]

It's the illusion of risk-free living. No matter what happens, you find that you can live happily ever after because money forms the safety net.

A sense of worthlessness and a lack of self-esteem. It's difficult to feel good about yourself, to sense you're really a competent, worthwhile person, if you have everything done for you. These feelings can be especially acute for those very wealthy adult children who don't even have to worry about getting a job.

Feelings of guilt. Sensitive children of the well-to-do often can't help making comparisons between their lot in life and that of the homeless and other unfortunates. When they see the disparities in material well-being, guilt can often emerge.

One man who inherited a million dollars said, "I'm still confronted with people sleeping in the streets. Money may filter that out, but it's not a shelter."

A tendency to hide one's wealth. One eleven-year-old boy from an upper-middle-class family in the Midwest was taken to Europe for several weeks by his parents—a privilege that wasn't available to most of his less affluent classmates. He enjoyed himself tremendously, but he felt uncomfortable when he returned to school and was asked by a teacher to report on the experience. He found himself trying to convince his peers that his family wasn't really *that* well-off, though he had to endure considerable kidding about being "rich." His main concern was that he just didn't want to be different from everybody else.

The temptation to deny their affluent heritage also overcomes those who are much wealthier than this boy. For example, George Pillsbury, heir of the flour fortune, regularly denied any link to his family when he was younger, and he avoided talking about expensive vacations. Similarly, Sewanee Hunt, daughter of Texas billionaire H. L. Hunt, hid her identity from her schoolmates and even moved to Europe to escape scrutiny.

Dating discomforts. Well-to-do girls and women may find that they have to play down their money when on a date so as not to intimidate a companion. Some men, of course, *prefer* rich women and are happy to share in their fortune. But others may feel that a woman with more money than they have somehow relegates them to an inferior role.

Both men and women of means may also begin to ask themselves, "Does she (he) like me for myself or for my money?" It's often hard, and may be quite impossible, to answer this question definitively. As a result, a relatively wealthy person may "freeze up" on a date or become so suspicious that he or she never makes a commitment.

An inability to manage inherited wealth. Quite often, I encounter children who have no idea about how to manage the money and material possessions that are handed over to them. Furthermore, this problem afflicts middle-class families as much as the very wealthy. Many times, loving, giving parents of modest means are determined to "give my child every advantage."

When a neighborhood child gets a personal computer or popular new toy car or action figure, the other children's parents also feel pressure to respond accordingly. In many ways, it's a variation on the old fallacy of "keeping up with the Joneses." I don't know how often I've heard adults deride this materialistic tendency to do as well and buy as much as friends and neighbors. Yet when it comes to their children, they don't hesitate to try to match acquisitions and other trappings of wealth.

Worst of all, these parents may shower their children with toys or other consumer goods and services indiscriminately, without providing accompanying instruction about how the money and possessions should be used. As a result, even the children of parents with limited resources may grow up as ill-prepared to deal with the real world and real money as those from very affluent homes.

The father of one of my young patients—a very open man with whom I could talk without beating around the bush—had inherited a great deal of money when his mother died. He had been only about twenty years old some ten years ago when he received the bequest of several million dollars. At the time, most of his friends, while sympathizing with him over the death of his parent, were secretly quite envious of what they regarded as his good fortune.

Yet simply receiving the money seemed to eliminate any drive or ambition this man had. He had always known he would come into a great deal of money, and so he had never really been "hungry" for financial success. When the estate finally became his, he became even less interested in honing his talents or applying his skills, either in the job market or in volunteer activities.

As we talked one evening, he delineated his feelings about his wealth. He said, "I could never measure up to my father, so what's the use of trying?" His father had been a self-made man, an extremely successful entrepreneur who had built up a string of businesses, which constituted the foundation of the family wealth.

"I know I have no goals in life, and frankly, I don't know how to establish any. There's really nothing I want to do or be," he readily admitted. And then he continued, "I see no point in going out and getting a job. After all, I don't need the money, and it seems a waste of time to spin my wheels in some boring office position."

Unfortunately, his undirected, lackadaisical approach to life was influencing his young son and daughter. They, too, were beginning to assume that life had no particular purpose or meaning. This lack of drive and focus was reflected in lower grades and great uncertainty about their own values, including what was right or wrong in their games, schoolwork, and relationships.

After a series of lengthy discussions, I concluded that a distorted response to money was at the root of the dissatisfaction in this man's life, so my advice to him was rather simple.

"Beginning right now, behave as though you have no money," I told him. "You're an intelligent person. You have many talents and a great deal of potential. But your money is stifling you. So just push it aside, at least for a few months or maybe even a year, and act like the rest of us! You may find you have to scramble to make ends meet. You may experience some anxieties. But these pressures and feelings will be much better for your emotional and physical health than what you're going through now."

How exactly could he "behave as though he had no money" or "push his money aside" for a few months or a year?

When he asked me these questions, I told him it wouldn't be easy. Nor did I have all the answers because I hadn't gone through what he was experiencing. But as we talked, the idea of walking away from his princely wealth for a while—in a manner reminiscent of the little ruler in Mark Twain's *The Prince and the Pauper*—became more and more appealing. Here is a summary of his strategy.

First, he put aside enough money so that he and his family could live comfortably for six months.

Next, he placed the rest of his money in a trust, with a provision that the income would not be paid to him or his family, at least not unless he took formal steps to change the terms of the trust. Instead, the earnings would be allowed to accumulate.

Finally, he began to regard himself as just another unemployed person, with enough money to make it through the next six months, but no more.

It was interesting to see the change in this man *and* in his children. He started talking about what sort of work he wanted to do and where he would look for possible positions. His son and daughter got into the rhythm of their dad's new approach to life, and they actually began to enjoy it. Furthermore, their interest in their schoolwork started picking up.

Overall, the simple act of *assuming* or *imagining* that they weren't wealthy had worked wonders in changing this family's attitude toward their money. Also, the father *did* finally secure a job—an accomplishment that raised his self-esteem considerably. The destructive marks and influences of too much money now disappeared almost completely.

Eventually, this man changed the terms of his trust so that he could dip into the accumulated earnings more easily. But he did so only after thinking long and hard about what he wanted to do with the money once he got his hands on it again.

Among other things, he developed a policy of philanthropy; he gave predetermined amounts to various charities and to his church. In the past, before he had begun to pretend that he wasn't rich, he had given almost no money away. He had only sat on his hoard, like some modern-day Scrooge. But now, he was able to experience the enjoyment of generosity and of sharing the financial blessings that had been given to him.

Also, he began to think more creatively about starting up projects to help others with his funds. One thing he did was to become the founder and primary contributor for a daily lunch program to feed the hungry and homeless in an area near where he worked.

Inherited wealth certainly doesn't have to be a gold-plated albatross that hangs around a person's neck, preventing constructive movement and promoting laziness and a lack of meaning. Money is meant to be *used* in exciting, beneficial ways, both for ourselves and for others. And the best time to start learning how to use it is in early childhood.

How Much Money Do You Spend on Your Child?

I frequently recommend, as the first phase in teaching a child about the wise use of money, that parents spend about a week compiling a list of approximately how much money is spent on the child. Everything—from food to school to camps to luxury items—should be included.

Note: Some of these items, such as food and shelter, may seem a little strange to put into this list because they're absolutely necessary expenses. You may feel, quite rightly, that there's no way to limit certain expenditures for your child. After all, you're certainly going to continue to provide him with something to eat and a roof over his head—regardless of what I suggest on teaching about the value of money!

But bear with me. At this point, I just want you to get a complete picture of your child's part of the total family income and expenses. You can decide later about what's a necessary expense and what's not.

In addition, by making this set of simple calculations, you'll be able to see more precisely the overall state of your family's finances. You need to know how much money you have available and where it's going. Only then can you make intelligent decisions about what good money management means in your particular family. Also, you'll get a better idea about what discretionary purchases are appropriate for your child.

Now, here's a step-by-step plan to determine the proportion of your family budget that's attributable to each child. Use the chart on page 00 to record the dollar figure called for in each step for each of your children. Then you will be able to calculate the total amount of family expenses generated by each child and the percentage of the family's income spent on discretionary expenses each month on each child.

Assume that each figure called for represents *one month's expenses.* For expenses paid as a lump sum—such as vacation and special entertainment outlays—figure the total yearly expenses in these categories and divide by twelve to get the expenses attributable to one month.

Step #1. Begin with the child's share of the rent or mortgage payments. This figure can be obtained by estimating the percentage of total housing space occupied by her room and play areas. Then, compute what dollar amount that percentage represents.

Step #2. Next, determine the child's approximate share in other joint household expenses, including telephone, insurance, electricity, and laundry. Probably, the child's share in each of these expenses should be the same as that of one adult. But there may be some variations from family to family. For example, the older the child, the larger his share in the telephone bill. Also, the more time he spends using electronic equipment, the greater his share of utility expenses.

Step #3. Determine the total amount you spend for food eaten at home. Count each child as one person, and figure out what proportion of the food expenses is attributable to him.

Step #4. Calculate the total amount you spend on *joint* family entertainment and vacations, excluding the purchase of gifts and mementos for individuals in the family. Count each child as one adult, and jot down the proportion of the expenditures attributable to him.

Step #5. Figure out what you spend on your child's essential clothing. At this point, exclude special or extra items of apparel.

With these first five calculations, you'll be able to cover most of your joint family expenses. Now, you should focus on expenditures that the child generates individually.

Step #6. Determine how much you spend on your child's non-basic clothing. This amount should include "extras," such as the additional pair of jeans or shoes that aren't really needed, and also special items, such as Halloween costumes, trendy party outfits, and jewelry.

Step #7. Determine how much you give your child for an allowance.

Step #8. Determine how much your child earns around the house doing chores.

Step #9. Calculate how much you spend on gifts for your child. Include Christmas and birthday gifts and also impulse purchases and purchases made on special occasions, such as entertainment outings or vacations. As with other lump sum expenses, add up all these gift expenses and divide by twelve to get the expenses attributable to one month.

Step #10. Figure out how much you spend per month on your child's schooling, including private school tuition and any special tutoring. Also, include items such as books and school supplies.

Step #11. List the amount you spend on camps and special summer or vacation programs. Find the total, and then divide by twelve for the monthly figure.

Step #12. How much do you spend on music lessons, sports programs, or other special instruction?

Step #13. Calculate how much your child spends on food out-side the home, including purchases made in fast-food restaurants, at street vendor stands, and the like.

Step #14. Finally, add in miscellaneous expenses and payments, such as those made when your youngster says, "Mom, can I have a couple of dollars for that magazine?"; "Dad, I'm going to the movies tonight, and I'm short a buck"; or "How about a pack of those base-ball cards?"

Now, add the expenses in Steps #1 through #5. These repre-sent most of the fundamental, necessary outlays that every parent must make for a child.

Next, add the expenses in Steps #6 through #14. For the most part, these are discretionary expenses. That is, they expand or contract, depending on the amount of money that the family has available.

Finally, figure the total expenses attributable to each child by adding the necessary expenses to the discretionary expenses.

Now, with these three sets of figures in front of you—along with your knowledge of your total family income and your total family expenses per month—you can begin to get an idea of how much money your child receives from the "family financial pot."

What do these figures mean? In general, I think that if you're spending less than 10 percent of your family's net income (after taxes) on extras for your child—those expenses indicated in Steps #6 through #14—you're probably on safe ground.

On the other hand, if you're spending 10 percent to 20 percent of your net income on these extras, you're skating on thin ice in terms of both your personal financial management and the messages about money you're sending to your child. And if you're spending *more* than 20 percent of your net income on the extras, you and your child are most likely already in big trouble with your understanding and application of sound principles of money management.

To understand these three levels of spending in concrete, dollars-and-cents terms, consider these examples.

A family with one daughter had an annual after-tax income of $40,000. They spent 5 percent of this income on their youngster for the extras described in Steps #6 through #14, or a total of about $2,000. (Remember that these outlays do *not* include expenditures for necessities like food, shelter, and basic clothing.) Consequently, they were well within the safe limits of spending on their child.

Proportion of Family Budget Spent on Each Child

	Names of Children				
Necessary Expenses					
#1 Housing	$	$	$	$	$
#2 Utilities					
#3 Food					
#4 Entertainment					
#5 Essential Clothing					
Monthly total of necessary expenses per child	$	$	$	$	$
Discretionary Expenses					
#6 "Extra" Clothing	$	$	$	$	$
#7 Allowance					
#8 Chores					
#9 Gifts					
#10 Education					
#11 Summer Activities					
#12 Extracurricular					
#13 Eating Out					
#14 Miscellaneous					
Monthly total of discretionary expenses per child	$	$	$	$	$
TOTAL MONTHLY EXPENSES PER CHILD	$	$	$	$	$
Percent of family's net income spent per month, per child on discretionary expenses (#6–#14).	%	%	%	%	%

Furthermore, simply by placing limits on their spending, they gave the girl an important message about the priorities and values in their lives. It's not that they were trying to say, "You're not important enough to us to warrant our spending more money on you." Far from it! Rather, these parents showed considerable warmth and attention toward their child; but they communicated their love through means other than money and material possessions.

A second family, with an after-tax income of about $50,000, spent 20 percent of their money on their two boys. This amounted to $10,000 a year, a burdensome sum, given the fact that the family had to pay for their mortgage, food, and other expenses from the remainder. Sometimes, the parents found they had to borrow money, usually through credit cards, to pay for all the extras. And they never were able to save anything.

A third family, with after-tax income of $60,000, spent one-third of their money, or $20,000 annually, on their son. Much of the money went into tuition for an expensive private school and high-priced summer camps. Also, these parents didn't skimp on buying their boy far more clothes and consumer goods than he needed, or on giving him pocket change whenever he asked for it.

As a result of these child-related expenditures, the family was constantly in debt, and in fact had sought debt counseling. Furthermore, both parents worked, and neither made much time for the boy during the week, though they did try to spend more time with him on weekends. Both mother and father felt guilty because of the lack of time they gave to their son, and they apparently tried to make up for it by showering things on him.

Few families with above-average incomes are like the first family I've described, but many resemble the second and third ones. I constantly encounter children who are suited up in high-priced clothing, such as a $50 or $100 party dress for a preschooler, which she'll outgrow in a matter of months. Or an eight-year-old with a $25 or $30 embroidered sweat shirt. Or a toddler in a $90 or $100 suit. Or children who have just gone to a birthday party that's cost parents anything from a few hundred to more than a thousand dollars. (One ad I came across from the big New York toy store, F.A.O. Schwarz, actually offered a "Birthday Party of a Lifetime" for a child and 13 friends for $18,000! And no, I *didn't* accidentally slip in an extra zero!)

Obviously, some of these figures are outlandish. But I imagine that certain of the costs of children's clothing that I've mentioned strike a responsive chord with many of you. Furthermore, I'm quite certain that many middle- and upper-middle-class parents are paying 10 percent to 20 percent or more of their after-tax income for extras for their children. And by almost any standard, that's too much, both for the family budget and for the child's value development.

So we know we often give our children too much money and too many things. But why do we do it? That's the key question that remains to be answered before we can begin to develop a sound financial strategy for kids.

Chapter Six

Why Parents Give Kids Too Much Money—and What You Can Do about It

Curing the Rich Kids Syndrome involves an understanding by the parents of why they have allowed the Syndrome to occur and the development of a strategy to attack the malady. Let's begin with the three main reasons that I've identified to explain why parents give their children too many things: (1) guilt; (2) substitutions for love; and (3) sloppy money-management habits.

Reason #1: Guilt.

As we've seen, there's a tendency these days for both parents to work—and to work long, intense hours. Unfortunately, children are often the losers when parents devote themselves to becoming winners in the pursuit of career goals. In far too many cases, working moms and dads don't have sufficient hours in the day to give their children the parenting time they need.

When these parents *do* find a few minutes at the end of a long working day, or perhaps a few hours on the weekends, they frequently lack the energy to give of themselves in the concentrated way their children need. I rarely meet working parents who have thought through a child-rearing strategy with the same thoroughness they think through a business project.

With a child, there's usually no clear or immediate payback—no commendation from a boss or promise of a raise or a promotion. Successful parenting requires less emphasis on short-term rewards and more emphasis on long-term efforts to influence a child's devel-opment. Also, plenty of patience is necessary to put up with the starts and stops, progressions and regressions, joys and frustrations, that inevitably accompany any human relationship.

Furthermore, these working mothers and fathers are usually acutely and painfully aware that they're falling short in the parent-hood role. They become anxious and upset when they perceive emo-tional, academic, and sometimes physical problems plaguing their children. They know, implicitly, without the advice of any child-care expert, that these problems are somehow related to the absence of a strong, authoritative caretaker—a role that usually must be filled by a mom or dad.

Yet even as these working parents recognize that there's a prob-lem, and as they begin to suspect that the source of the difficulty involves their absence from their children's lives, they are caught in a bind. They want to help their children; they desperately desire to be with them more. But they ask, "How can I possibly give up my job or cut back on my career goals? I've worked too hard to get where I am now!"

So they begin to rationalize: "I'll be able to put in more time with Suzy later, when I've moved further along in my career" or "We have a good baby sitter who can give Joe all he needs during the day."

Sometimes, there may be truth in these statements; but more often, they arise out of a huge dose of wishful thinking. What your child needs most is *you*—that is, he or she needs the *you* who is able to put in the time, thought, and commitment necessary to be a good parent.

Many parents decide that they're going to "have it all." They're going to be parents *and* totally committed career persons. As the result of such a parental attitude, the children get shortchanged. The parents, knowing they're not giving enough of themselves or their time, feel guilty about their inadequacies. So they try to compensate with material possessions.

This approach, which is never as crassly stated or thought about as in the terms I'm about to use, may nevertheless be summarized fairly accurately like this: "I can't give enough of myself. And that makes me feel guilty because I know I'm doing less for my child's development than I should be doing. So to make up for my lack of time and energy—and to assuage my guilt—I'll provide her with more money . . . or more toys . . . or more 'opportunities' like special classes and activities."

I know one four-year-old who has everything money can buy. Her mother literally buys her whatever she asks for, either on the spot or, without fail, at the next major gift-giving occasion, such as a birthday or Christmas. Money is no obstacle for this child, first of all because the mother and father live under a constant pall of guilt. They are driven to compensate for that guilt by giving far too many things to their youngster. Also, the parents, who have high-paying jobs, can afford any fantasy that a four-year-old imagination can come up with.

A typical scenario in this family unfolds with the four-year-old saying, "Mommy, can I have that stuffed bear?"

The mother replies, "Now you know, Janie, that you really don't need another stuffed toy."

"I really *do* need that one, Mommy! Please, please give it to me! I really *have* to have it!"

Finally, Mommy gives in, primarily because she wants to show her love for Janie in every way that she can. Also, she feels a little guilty because, as I've said, she holds down a job and is away from home a great deal. As a result, when Mom is around Janie, she wants to do everything for the girl she possibly can. Often, that means showering gifts on her daughter.

Unfortunately, what this mother and other parents like her fail to take into account is the impact that this excessive gift-giving can have on a child's attitude toward money and physical possessions. Frequently, the child gets used to *getting;* but she rarely is taught anything about giving and sharing. Some altruistic qualities may develop naturally in the child, but more often, she tends to become possessive and also develops the belief that she really *deserves* the material things that constantly are showered on her.

Gifts may be used to take away the pain of loneliness; they take the place of emotional involvement. Parental "involvement" seems to have primarily monetary expressions rather than normal emotional interaction. Also, children like Janie begin to assume, because of the example projected by their parents, that giving things is an important and perhaps even essential part of showing love and affection. After all, if your mom and dad gave things to you to show how much they cared, you should receive the same from others, such as friends or a spouse. Conversely, if the friends or spouse don't give you things, the assumption is often that you are not liked or loved.

(Many children in this situation, both as youngsters and as adults, don't take the next step in this line of thinking. They don't always assume that *they* should give things to others to show their love—at least not unless they feel guilty and need to rely on money as a means to assuage these feelings.)

Reason #2: Things as a substitute for love.

One pair of yuppie parents came to see me for help because their little girl, a seven-year-old who was an only child, had developed a problem with bed-wetting. Also, the youngster wasn't doing well in school.

As I questioned the parents, they revealed that they were both working professionals who were frequently away from home. When they did return from a long day at the office or from a trip, they usually would bring the youngster a present of some sort. These gifts became a kind of reward or compensation paid to the child because the parent had not been able to be present. The parents further thought that by bringing a gift, they were including her in their work life and demonstrating how they thought of her while away.

But unlike the family described previously, this mother and father didn't harbor any feelings of guilt. They thought their lives and priorities were in good order. As they saw it, they were giving their child all the time they could spare, and it was perfectly acceptable to make up for what they couldn't do with a special gift.

It was immediately apparent to me, however, that they were fooling themselves. They had fallen into the habit of substituting inanimate objects for an adequate relationship with their daughter.

The girl soon became accustomed to ask, "Where's my toy?" when one of the adults failed to pick up an item for her. She also began to link these material items with her relationship with her parents. The child sensed, quite rightly, that the parents regarded the gifts as substitutes for a real relationship, so she came to attach a huge importance to them.

Obviously, the presents were an inappropriate exchange for real human contact. Feeling this void in her life, which had arisen because of a lack of needed parent-child contact, the girl had begun to develop emotional and physical symptoms—an inability to concentrate on her schoolwork and also bed-wetting.

As I worked with this family, we explored ways that the parents might be able to spend more time with their daughter. They finally worked out a way to include an extra hour or so each day with the girl, though this change in their schedule took some sacrifice on the part of the parents. The demands on them at work were such that long hours were a prerequisite to promotions and salary raises. But these are just some of the hard choices that must be made when children receive too much in the way of mateiral possessions and too little in the way of warm, parental contact.

Reason #3: Sloppy money management.

One of the most common factors that causes parents to set up situations where their children have too much money is sloppy personal financial practices. Often, for example, it's easier to give the child the money he requests than it is to enter into a lengthy discussion or argument. It's sometimes just too much of a bother to explain why impulse purchases are bad or why granting the request would violate the family budget or the like.

Also, many families don't have clearly formulated budgets or personal financial principles that they operate under. They buy items with credit cards when the urge strikes, and in general they operate on the "buy now, pay later" philosophy. So when it is time to respond to a request by a child, the tendency is just to treat that request as another necessary demand on them as consumers and to react accordingly by paying up.

Finally, there's a tendency for loving parents—even those who aren't motivated by guilt or the search for love substitutes—to want to give as much to their children as possible. They accede to children's requests out of love, without setting up any priorities about which purchases or gifts are important for the children and which ones are not.

I recall one mother and father, quite typical of many parents I encounter, who had run into financial difficulties because of unwise use of their credit cards and personal bank lines of credit. They weren't yet ready to declare bankruptcy, but they were deeply in debt. It wasn't at all clear how they were going to get out of the financial hole they had dug for themselves.

They consulted me because they had been advised to cut back on many of their expenditures, including exorbitant purchases for their two children. (They were in the category of parents who spend more than 20 percent of their after-tax income on extras for their children, such as excessive numbers of toys, expensive summer camps, high-priced clothing, and private schools.)

They knew they had to do something to bring their personal budget into balance and begin to retire their debts. But they were afraid that if they cut back on their children's material advantages, the youngsters might suffer emotionally or physically.

"I'm worried that they might become insecure," the mother said. "I've heard so much about children developing emotional problems because of insecure situations at home, and I don't want to expose them to anything like that. Also, what about physical problems that might develop if we deny them things, like certain camps or clothing? Should we worry about that?"

I assured them that their two girls, who were seven and ten years old, were well-adjusted and unlikely to be hurt by the loss of the material things that had been bestowed on them.

"In fact, they might be better off," I said. "You've obviously had a problem with your personal budget, and that's been a bad example for these children. They thought they could have anything— that every day was Christmas. But this is a misconception that could do them much more harm in the future than simply learning the truth right now: that there are limits and should be limits on what we can buy.

"Now, you have a great opportunity to set them on a more productive track. As you address your financial problems, perhaps you should explain to your children some of the things you're doing so that they learn these skills, too. You don't have to disclose all your balance sheets and income statements to them. Nor do you have to let them know every time you experience a fleeting worry or anxiety about money. They wouldn't understand, and communicating each little concern probably wouldn't help them.

"On the other hand, you *can* show them some basic principles about how to set up their own budgets. You can instruct them in how to balance the income they receive from their allowances and odd jobs against their expenses, and how to set money aside for savings and for charitable giving."

I knew this was a churchgoing family, and the idea of arranging the children's finances so that there was money left over for church was appealing. Also, the parents were reassured to know that it would be more beneficial for their children to participate in the financial belt-tightening than to be left out or ignored during this crisis.

How did this mother and father teach their children more about the value of money? In the following section, I've outlined a plan that parents can use to instruct their children about the value of money and the best use of material possessions.

A Money-Management Strategy for Kids Who Have Too Much

As I see it, six major principles are the foundation for a wise money-management strategy for children. By promoting and following each of these principles in the family, parents should find that they end up with kids who do *not* have too much. Rather, the children will know how to use and rely on their money and material possessions in ways that reflect broader, more authentic values.

Principle #1: Present the true value of money to your child.

A wise money-management strategy for children must begin with the communication of a balanced philosophy of wealth. Money is something, but it's not everything in life. Yet many parents live as though their money and material possessions were the most important things in the world, and children are quick to pick up on these priorities. So you must make it a point to *tell* your child what you believe the true value of money is; and you must also *show* that through your actions and example.

Of course, all this assumes that you really do have a personal philosophy of wealth. If you don't—if you find that you spend indiscriminately or without a definite idea of how your purchases fit into your family budget—this is the time to establish a more sound personal money-management system. There's no way to teach your child the proper value of money unless you possess good personal financial values.

I realize that every set of parents will approach their money and material things a little differently. Some may relate their approach to money to a religious faith. Others may have a sense that their assets should be shared as much as possible with those less fortunate—a personal share-the-wealth philosophy. Still others may put a primary emphasis on a hard-work ethic, which stresses that money and assets are direct results of how much effort is put into a job. I know some people who combine these three sets of values.

Several considerations determined the money-management values of one Christian family I encountered recently. The parents followed these guidelines and also taught them to their children.

All that we own was given to us by God. Therefore, we are in effect stewards, or managers, of our material goods and money. Every time this family prayed together, either during devotionals or at the dinner table, the parents mentioned this point.

Because God has blessed us with material things—and because those things are really His, not ours—*we have a responsibility to return a portion* of our possessions and income to God for His work in the world.

Specifically, this family chose the traditional route of tithing, or giving 10 percent of their income to their church, as a means of returning part of their income to God's work. Also, they gave additional money to charitable activities in their community, including programs designed to help needy children and families. Whenever possible, they combined personal contact with the giving of money, canned goods, or toys to these children.

The children in the family participated in this sharing. They donated 10 percent of their allowances and earned money to their church, and they also selected the toys or other items that they wanted to donate to the less fortunate boys and girls.

Hard work is a high virtue and should be rewarded. In addition to their emphasis on giving to others, the parents encouraged the younger children, who were six and nine years old, to do special chores around the house as a means to earn extra money.

Responsibilities like cleaning up their rooms were *not* regarded as jobs that entitled children to extra money; rather, the chores were part of each child's expected behavior as a member of the family. On the other hand, helping with the general house cleaning or yard work could earn them varying amounts of money. The oldest child, a teenager, did yard work and baby sitting for neighbors to earn extra cash.

Obviously, not every family will affirm these precise values.

But many others will. The significant thing is to think through your personal philosophy of life, decide how material possessions fit into it, and then live according to that philosophy—and encourage your child to do likewise.

Principle #2: Give your child an allowance—with no strings attached.

Most financial advisers recommend that at least part of the money a child receives from parents should be given unconditionally. In other words, the child shouldn't have to earn the basic allowance, nor should he be threatened with a loss of allowance if he misbehaves.

There are a couple of good reasons for this no-strings-attached approach, at least for a part of the money a youngster receives.

First, if you make a child work for every penny she receives and attach monetary value to a wide variety of actions and behaviors, money can assume too much importance in the child's mind. A child isn't supposed to hold down a full-time job. Her parents have brought her into the world with the understanding that she will depend on them for years, usually until she approaches adulthood. Part of the security and support that a parent provides for a child should be financial, and the child should understand that during her period of dependency, she is a participant, without conditions, in the family assets.

I realize that this point may seem to be in tension with, or even to contradict, what I've been saying about not giving kids too much. But actually, no conflict exists at all. There's nothing wrong with giving your children money and gifts, without expecting anything in return. In fact, I believe it's a good example to show children that you love them enough to unconditionally give them material things as well as your love and time. The problem arises, *not* when you give them a reasonable gift or sum of money, but when you give them too much.

Second, if parents begin to play unpleasant games with their child's allowance, such as withholding part of it as a punishment, an undesirable message is communicated. The child is led to understand that money can and should be used as a club, to coerce certain conduct or to sanction certain bad behavior.

Think about the implications. There's the wife who refuses to pool the money she has earned with the rest of the family income and assets "until my husband can learn to manage his finances better." Or the divorced man who resists making regular alimony payments "because she doesn't deserve that much." Or the individual who has contracted for a certain business service, but then withholds payments that are legally and rightfully due to a contractor "because I want him to do a little extra on this job for me."

Such attitudes are destructive to relationships and may even get the perpetrators in hot legal water. Too often, adults who approach their money in these ways have learned these negative habits when they were much younger. So now is the time, when your children are still children, to inculcate more productive attitudes in them.

How much of an allowance should you give a child? That's up to the particular family's financial situation, the age of the child, and the area in which they live. But there are some general guidelines. A 1988 survey in *Working Mother* magazine revealed that the average allowance for a five-year-old is $1.40 a week; a sixteen-year-old, in contrast, averages $8.13 a week.

Principle #3: Teach your child that hard, efficient work will bring material rewards.

In our society there's a prevalent worry that too many people are lazy or on some sort of dole. In other words, the welfare mentality—the expectation of something for nothing—has run rampant. According to this thinking, even individuals who work at regular jobs often lack a commitment to diligence and excellence in executing their assigned tasks.

I agree it's a good idea to teach children that there's a positive relationship between hard work and money. Two ways of accomplishing this, which I've discovered to be beneficial to the emotional and physical health of youngsters, are (1) being paid for doing special jobs around the house and (2) earning income from part-time jobs in the community.

Jobs around the house. As I've already mentioned, most experts seem to feel that you shouldn't pay a child every time he makes his bed or brushes his teeth. That puts too much emphasis on money and too little on the fact that not everything we do should have a price tag.

On the other hand, many parents have been successful in giving their children a relatively modest unconditional allowance and then providing for supplementary cash through a program of household chores. Each family must come up with an individual program, which will be based on the special home situation and also on the particular financial values that the family espouses.

For example, one family gives the older son, who is thirteen, a small allowance. In addition, he can earn extra money by mowing the yard, shoveling snow, washing the family car, and doing other such jobs. The boy is paid the "going rate" for these jobs, and he's expected to live up to his commitments as well as he would on any job.

He understands that if he says he's going to do the yard work for one season, and then he neglects it, he may lose the job to another child in the neighborhood who wants the work. There's an additional, built-in incentive for him to abide by his "contract" with his parents because he knows they won't hand out extra money to him for a movie or another personal expense if he fails to earn it.

Part-time jobs in the community. Even as I applaud systems like the one I just mentioned, I worry sometimes about the tendency of youngsters these days to take on too much outside work. A number of studies have been done on the so-called work-spend ethic that has arisen among many teenagers—a trend that involves spending a lot of extracurricular time at jobs in order to earn money for excessive purchases.

There are some big problems with this trend. First of all, children who work too much at an early age often find that they don't have time for other activities that will be much more vital to them in the long run than the money they earn right now. Many such children neglect their homework and get worse grades than they're capable of. They also typically eschew extracurricular activities, such as sports, science projects, speech contests, musical instruction, and the like. Yet these activities and skills may be *extremely* important in positioning them for admission to good colleges and in enabling them to lead richer, more interesting lives as adults.

Another drawback to too much work is the tendency to lose sleep, eat poorly, and experience work-related anxieties too soon. One fifteen-year-old boy was referred to me by his parents because of a number of complaints. He had developed regular stomach upsets; he frequently woke up with headaches; and he always seemed tired. Also, his grades had been suffering to the extent that his parents were afraid he might not get into college at all.

When I questioned him about what he was doing with his time after school, the source of the problem became clear. He was working in three part-time jobs—a fast-food restaurant during the week; a shoe store on weekends; and baby-sitting chores one weekend night each week. By my calculations, he was averaging less than five hours of sleep a night. That was clearly one of the sources of his fatigue.

Also, he was preoccupied with pressures associated with his jobs. How would he deal with an unfair boss at the fast-food place? How could he find relief from some of the pressures from impatient customers during those hours when traffic at the restaurant became especially heavy? Should he continue to sit for one set of young children who were particularly unruly?

These worries and pressures seemed the most likely candidates for the source of the stomach problems the boy was experiencing. Yet when I suggested that he cut back on his part-time work, he immediately objected, "I couldn't possibly give anything up. I need the money! I've got a steady girl friend, and I like to go out at least once a week with my friends to a movie or something. Also, I buy a lot of extra clothes with that money. How would I pay for all that?"

In ensuing discussions with this boy and his parents, we worked out a solution that involved raising his no-strings-attached allowance and reducing his work commitments. At the same time, the boy had to reconcile himself to the fact that he would have to operate on a reduced budget.

He didn't like the idea at first. But finally, he began to understand that he was hurting his health and also putting himself at a disadvantage for the future with his bad academic performance. He agreed to this program and soon found that he actually liked the more relaxed pace of life. Just as important, his stomach problems and headaches disappeared; his energy returned; and his grades improved markedly.

When I consider such cases, I see clearly that there are limits to how far you can go in teaching a child the value of money through outside work. Some pay-for-work experience is certainly desirable, but too much can open the back door to the very problem we're trying to solve here—the kid who has too much money.

Principle #4: Show your child how to save.

A fundamental part of any instruction in money management is to teach a child the importance of saving. There are several simple but effective ways to go about this.

For young children, such as those still in the early years of elementary school, it's helpful to firmly encourage them to set aside a certain percentage of their allowance—say, 10 percent—for savings. So if a child gets an allowance of two dollars a week, he would put twenty cents (or a quarter, if that's easier for the child to deal with) into a piggy bank or other savings container.

The child should be encouraged to set a relatively long-term goal for the savings. For example, he might accumulate money to buy some special toy. Or he might want to get an article of clothing that doesn't fit into the parents' budget. Or the goal might be an expensive piece of sports equipment, like a baseball glove. Some children may even be satisfied with saving for the sake of saving—for the satisfaction of seeing their "pot" or "estate" grow larger and larger.

It's also instructive to set up a savings account for the child, with the parent as custodian. Then, when the monthly statements arrive from the bank, the parent can show the child how much money he has and how the interest is accumulating.

One father who set up such an account for a seven-year-old son would say, "Look, this month you earned seven dollars in interest at the bank. And what did you have to do to earn that money?"

"Nothing," the boy replied. He knew from what his father had already told him that the *money* was earning the interest for him in the bank account.

As children get older and more adept in mathematics, they should be taught the power of compound interest. Tables obtained from a bank or a money-management book will show clearly how much money can be earned just by leaving a sum in a bank account over a long period of time.

One recent article I read indicated that if a person invested $2,000 yearly between ages of twenty-one and thirty at 8 percent annual interest, the compound effect would give her more than $600,000 in the account by the time she was sixty-five!

You'll probably be dealing with much smaller figures for your child. But still, it can make a dramatic impact to work up an example of compound interest to fit your youngster's situation.

For older children, aged ten and above, an investment program established in a brokerage house can be quite educational. One father set up an investment account for his eleven-year-old son by introducing the boy to his own stockbroker and having the boy choose a couple of stocks to buy.

This youngster had already saved several hundred dollars over a period of years in a savings account, and his father agreed to put up a matching sum. Then, the boy chose his stocks from some companies that particularly interested him—a toy company and a sporting goods manufacturer. He learned that he had enough money to buy the stocks in "whole lots" (one-hundred-share amounts) and that this approach would save him brokerage commissions. As he proceeded, he also acquired a considerable amount of practical financial knowledge that stood him in good stead as he grew older.

Principle #5: Encourage your child to give money to worthy causes that have a strong personal quality.

It's almost impossible for a child to be motivated to give his precious money to a "worthy cause"; at least, it's impossible if the cause isn't somehow linked to a particular human consideration.

For example, you might draw a blank with your son or daughter if you say, "Let's contribute to this foreign mission program, which will help sick people overseas." But if you say, "You see that poor man standing over there? Let's give some money that's going to help him," you're likely to get a favorable response from the child.

Of course, this fund-raising approach works for adults, too. It's always more effective to get someone to give to needy people he or she can see than it is to secure a contribution to building maintenance or some other impersonal or abstract appeal.

How you personalize your child's giving is a very individual issue, and doing it successfully will probably take some creativity on your part as a parent. But believe me, it's worth the effort. The tender, generous side of children often goes untapped and unnurtured because adults don't devote the time or thought to develop an attractive strategy of giving.

Principle #6: Help your child become wise in the ways of modern-day marketing and advertising.

Much has been said and written in recent years about the bad influence of marketing and advertising techniques on children. But this trend is likely to continue because there are some good reasons why businesses are targeting children as a major market.

For one thing, children have a lot of money to spend. Those aged nine to twelve spend almost *all* of the $4.73 billion they receive annually through allowances, gifts, and other earnings, according to a 1984 study by James U. McNeal, a Texas A&M University professor. Also, McNeal says these children "are directly influencing parental spending of over $40 billion a year."[1]

A survey by Yankelovich, conducted with the Nickelodeon children's cable network and *USA Today,* found that 23 percent of children aged six to fifteen cook their own meals at least part of the time, and six percent cook most of the time. Other studies have revealed that 50 percent of all teenage girls shop once a week for family groceries; and 55 percent of all children in the Yankelovich study said they choose different grocery brands from those their parents do.

Such reports suggest that parents should pay close attention to teaching their children constructive ways to respond to marketing and advertising campaigns, both for the children's *and* for the parents' sakes! If a child usually has a positive, uncritical response to seductive advertising, that child is extremely vulnerable to using his money to buy what the seller is pushing. On the other hand, if the child has learned to ask key questions of the ads before he responds positively, he'll be in a much stronger position as a consumer.

Some possible queries you might suggest your child ask herself before she responds to an advertising pitch include the following:

▶ What does this product they're selling *really* look like? What does it *really* do? How can I find out?

▶ Am I likely to get fooled if I order something that's advertised on TV and then have it sent to me through the mail?

▶ Is it possible to return the item if I don't like it? If so, what are the rules for returning it?

▶ How will I use the product if I buy it?

▶ What will I be unable to buy if I spend my money on this item?

You can probably think of many additional questions. These are just a few to get you started and to stimulate your child's critical faculties. Nobody, including the typical child, likes to be fooled or pushed into doing something silly or stupid. So if you can get your son or daughter to understand that certain types of advertising and marketing are designed to do just that, the youngster will be much less likely to be duped or to spend money unwisely.

The use and abuse of money in a family is obviously a very complex and difficult issue. There's no single formula or rigid set of rules that will ensure success in this area, for each family's needs, income level, and interests are different. But with a little prior goal setting and budgetary planning—and a great deal of understanding and love between parents and children—there's every reason to expect a situation where your kids have *just enough* money and material goods.

Chapter Seven

Kids Who Have Too Much Pressure to Perform

Modern-day parents put plenty of pressure on their children to achieve, achieve, achieve. Being a high-performance individual is, in many ways, the late twentieth-century equivalent of what being a good, upright, honest, or moral person was a few decades ago.

Also, the accelerated pace of living in our high-tech society has increased the variety of opportunities and sources of stimulation for today's children. As a result, there are a variety of practical programs supposedly designed to get a child started on the road to becoming a concert-level musician, an Olympic athlete, or a highly educated, high-earning professional.

Aware of all these opportunities, promises, and pressures to perform, many parents assume that they had better get their children on the fast-track, high-achievement bandwagon as soon as possible, or the kids will lose out. They'll fail to reach their full potential, and the fault for failure will be laid squarely at the feet of Mom and Dad!

Some parents may say to themselves, "Hey, I have a chance here to *live again* through my children, and I can do it with society's full approval! My parents made a lot of mistakes with me, but I can make up for them through these new programs and methods."

But usually, when parents get caught up in approving or even promoting this pressure on their children to perform, something goes wrong. More often than not, they find that children can't be programmed to move successfully along a road to high achievement that has been mapped out by parents.

One music professor at a major university was quite happy to find that his young son had some significant musical talent. The adult became determined to give the seven-year-old boy opportunities that he felt he had missed while he was growing up.

Specifically, the father believed his parents had started him on his music lessons too late. He had been about ten years old when he began taking piano. Also, they hadn't really emphasized the importance of long hours of practice because they had not had any idea that he might become a concert-level pianist.

This father's perception of the way his parents had handled him led him to believe he had missed out on a career as a famous, performing musician. As he saw it, he had been forced to settle for second best, the role of a teacher. But he resolved that this wasn't going to be the fate of his child, at least not if he could help it!

In addition to the musical talent that the father saw in the boy, the youngster's mother thought she discerned physical coordination that might lead to excellence in athletics. In particular, when she had the boy swing a tennis racquet a few times, she noticed that the child seemed to have superior hand-to-eye coordination. So, the boy was set to begin the music regimen planned by the father and tennis lessons arranged by the mother.

But as often happens, these well-laid strategies by the parents didn't quite work out as expected. After about a year of pushing the child to stick with the athletic and musical programs, the father and mother became extremely frustrated. Finally, the parents and child made an appointment with me because the boy had begun to complain of regular stomachaches and headaches. He had been missing school frequently because of these ailments, and he had also had to skip many of his music and tennis lessons.

The parents were quite worried about the boy's health. But they were also clearly concerned that he was getting behind the personal development schedule they had established for him. "Time is passing by!" the father said, although his son had just turned nine years of age.

I examined the boy thoroughly, but I couldn't find anything physically wrong with him—other than the fact that he was complaining of certain aches and pains. I began to suspect that there was a deeper emotional source for the physical difficulties.

As we talked, the full scope of his underlying resistance to the music and sports emerged. It soon became apparent that something had to be done to change the situation and relieve the pressure on the boy. Otherwise, much more serious physical and emotional consequences might result.

I told these parents directly that they were putting too much pressure on their son. "You *have* to let up!" I said. "It's important for this child to have *fun* participating in his music and sports. After all, he's barely nine!"

I emphasized to them that he was still emotionally and physically a child, and he wasn't prepared to forge ahead in the music and sports fields with a hard-driving adult mentality. "He's not a professional, and if he ever becomes one, that time is years away," I said.

In fact, I said, if adult pressures and demanding adult standards continued to be imposed on the youngster, it was almost certain that one or both of two undesirable results would occur: Either he would develop more serious health problems, or he would react completely against these skills and activities that were so dear to his parents.

This mother and father agreed to back off and let the boy develop in a more relaxed and natural way, without any overbearing pressure to perform according to preconceived adult standards. As a result, their son actually began to *like* to practice his music and his sports! His father was often present with him during the music sessions, and both parents participated in tennis whenever possible. Without the pushing and the pressure, the youngster found he really liked the parental companionship.

On the other hand, it wasn't so easy for the parents to change their old habits. When the boy made a mistake or seemed to be giving less than his best, he might receive a criticism or lengthy instruction that he didn't want to hear. Invariably, that sort of pushing from the parent would cause a rebellious, negative reaction in the son; and the particular practice session or outing would abruptly end in an unproductive and tense confrontation.

When I last contacted this family, the son's interest in tennis had intensified. He had been doing quite well in informal tennis matches, and also he had performed well in a couple of tournaments. In addition, he was doing a creditable job as a pianist.

However, he certainly wasn't at concert level with his music. Furthermore, despite the progress he had been making with his tennis, he wasn't the best in his age group—and he might never be. But at least he was developing well at his own pace. Most important of all, he and his parents were enjoying life much more.

The trap that these parents had fallen into—and been rescued from—is known as *hothousing*. This contemporary fallacy in child-rearing needs further explanation.

Is Your Home a Hothouse?

Child psychologists and educators, in observing the trend in the last decade or so toward creating superbabies and otherwise pushing children to perform, have used the term *hothousing* to refer to this phenomenon.

A real hothouse, of course, is a greenhouse, often for growing tropical plants, which is kept at a relatively high temperature with little of the environmental change usually found outdoors. In a similar vein, parents who try to establish a high-pressure, highly controlled environment to nurture maximum performance and achievement are said to be hothousing their youngsters. Rather than let their children grow and develop their skills at a more relaxed pace, the adults try to accelerate learning and get their sons and daughters off to a faster start than everyone else.

Think about your home. Do you sense you've been involved in hothousing your child? To evaluate your situation, consider the following evidences or signs that hothousing may be at work.

Sign #1: Most of your child's day is booked up.

When I encounter a family where the children have to move from one activity directly to the next, with little or no time for free play, I know I'm looking at a possible hothousing environment.

What happens if an event scheduled according to split-second timing is delayed? The pressure to "catch up" with the original schedule may become oppressive. All children, especially young ones, *must* have at least an hour or two each day for their own creative play. Being free to indulge in imaginative expression is part of developing intelligence. Also, it's essential for everyone, adult or child, to have some time alone just to decompress and find relief from the pressures of daily life.

I'm not saying that it's wrong or unwise to keep your child busy and expose him to a variety of special education programs. But I do believe that parents must exercise plenty of discretion and be very careful not to overbook a child. If your child has too little free time, the chances are she will begin to show physical or emotional signs of stress—a topic we'll deal with more in the next section.

Sign #2: A toddler or prekindergarten child is enrolled in one or more early formal instruction programs.

From 1970 to 1986, enrollment in early educational programs, including those offered by private and public institutions, increased from just over 4 million to more than 6 million children. But a growing number of child development experts are questioning this trend.

For example, Edward Zigler, a Yale psychologist who was director of child development for the Department of Health, Education and Welfare under President Nixon, has concluded that this early instruction has "no long-term effect on middle-class kids."[1]

Others argue that starting a two-and-a-half- or three-year-old on violin or piano, as programs such as the Suzuki method do, isn't helpful for later performance. A similar criticism is leveled at programs that attempt to start children swimming as "water babies" at eighteen months or introduce them to math or advanced vocabulary at early ages.

Although I become concerned sometimes about these tendencies, I think it's important to deal with each child as an individual. It's necessary to discern whether a particular child is ready for—and, more important, really *enjoys*—an early educational program. Also, it's essential for parents to sort through their own motives. Ask yourself, "Am I starting Mikey in this program because *he's* interested, or because *I* am?"

You may question whether a toddler or preschooler is in a position to tell a parent whether or not he's interested in something. But I think children are more capable of letting parents know something about their interests and abilities than many people realize.

It's helpful to ask, Is the child exploring a variety of interests simultaneously and then returning to one for a special focus? Too much pressure to engage in *every* activity at full throttle negates the fun of experimenting and choosing activities that will be of greatest interest later.

Some children, for instance, will take to a musical instrument at a very young age. Olegna Fuschi, director of the Juilliard School's precollege division in Manhattan, seems to be a case in point. She actually started taking piano lessons at the incredibly young age of eighteen months! Yet she doesn't appear to have been moved along too quickly in this area by her parents, who apparently perceived a natural interest and responded to it.

Both her parents were musicians, and so the temptation must have been almost overwhelming for them to push their daughter. But they let her proceed at her own pace.

"My mother was very careful with me," Fuschi says. "She started by only letting me spend maybe five minutes a day at the piano. But whatever I did was correct. It wasn't just random—it was precise. I worked hard, but I enjoyed practicing."[2]

It appears that these parents were onto something. Fuschi continued with the piano and rose to a high level in the musical field. But I wouldn't take her example as a model that most parents should follow. Rather, the lesson to be learned here is that your child undoubtedly has a talent or interest in which he may be able to excel. But the talent may not be something that you expect. Or if you do expect it, your child may not be able or inclined to move along at the pace that you select.

So if you do enroll your son or daughter in an early educational program, be sure that you listen to the child's response. If he isn't having a good time, or if you sense you're the one who is pushing and your child is mostly resisting, it may be best to pull back and try again at a later time, if at all.

Sign #3: The parent enrolls the child, at whatever age, in programs designed to provide a special advantage over other youngsters.

Again, there's nothing inherently wrong with the practice of putting your youngster in a special instruction program. I'm all for giving tennis lessons to a child who is drawn to the sport at age seven or eight. Similarly, a young computer whiz may thrive at a computer camp during the summer.

A problem arises, however, if you *force* a child to take tennis lessons when the sport repels or bores him or if you pack him away to computer camp when he really wants to go fishing and hiking somewhere. This sort of pushiness and pressure to perform in ways that don't come naturally or happily to the child is what you want to avoid.

Life for the child isn't a talent contest; nor should it be a competition to get a prize for coming in first. Forcing the production of a Renaissance child may look good to school admission committees. But this will do little to help a child find the best path to live a fulfilling life.

Take reading as another illustration. Some parents are eager to have their children start reading before everyone else, and certainly before they reach first grade. Yet Dr. David Elkind, president of the National Association for the Education of Young Children, believes that children aren't developmentally ready to learn how to read until about age six and a half.

The same principle applies to early math education. "Parents think if their children are not multiplying by age four, they won't get into Harvard by age 18," says William Kristol, a Harvard professor and former chief of staff to U.S. Education Secretary William J. Bennett under former President Reagan. "Our sense is that the evidence does not support that. There's too much pressure on parents."

Not to mention pressure on the children. Kristol goes on to say that "leading child development experts have expressed reservations about putting four- and five-year-olds under too much pressure or into formal classroom settings."[3]

The result of this excessive early education pressure may be "burnouts" among children who seem to do well at a very young age, but then lose steam and interest by age ten or eleven.

"I'm seeing kids in second and third grade being referred for attention problems and hyperactivity as a result of being stressed and being expected to do things they're not ready to do," Tulsa pediatrician Robert Block told a *Wall Street Journal* reporter. "They're in a sphincter-tightening, teeth-grinding kind of environment. You see them in class and their mouths are twisted, their tongues are out, they're sweating a little."[4]

As children get older, the pressure from parents to perform and achieve may escalate, especially as the college years draw near. One recent movement involves the hiring of tutors by many well-to-do and middle-class parents to give their children an edge in college admissions. With this approach, the children continue with their regular school classes; in addition, they spend regular hours with tutors in an effort to increase their academic performance to maximum levels. As a supplement, there are also many books, computer programs, and classes designed specifically to improve students' performance on the SAT (Scholastic Aptitude Test).

In other words, these parents don't send their children to tutors just to help them pass courses. Rather, according to Judith Langer, a professor of education at the State University of New York at Albany, "B students are there to become A students and A students to become A+ students. I think there's been a change in values in the American social system. There's greater stress among the middle class to be part of the upper class. Getting your child into a good college is part of that process."[5]

Tutoring is a costly alternative to regular education. Parents may pay as much as forty dollars an hour for this service. Some critics have argued that the ability of the affluent to hire tutors gives an unfair advantage to those with money. I'm not as worried about this perceived advantage as I am about the pressures that the extra academic load puts on the student. Tutoring may be appropriate for some children, but certainly not all.

These descriptions of and concerns about high-pressured educational techniques reflect what I've encountered in my experience with children and parents. And what is all the pushing and nudging of youngsters leading to? The major result of putting too much pressure on a child is stress; and the consequences of stress on a young person's mental and physical health can be devastating.

The Consequences of Childhood Stress

Both physical and emotional consequences of stress may show up in children. Before we get to the specific symptoms, though, let me summarize some of the possible "stressors" that may be at the root of various problems.

Encouraging children to grow up too early

An emphasis on early education, including the intake of excessive amounts of information, often squeezes out traditional childhood. Or as child psychologist Lawrence Balter of New York

University says, the innocent world of childhood is "gone. Children have been 'adultified.' These are stressful times for kids."[6]

Specifically, through television and other means, children are introduced at too young an age to sex, money worries, violence, and other stressful concepts and events. Sitcoms and movies portray children as miniature adults, with preschoolers and elementary school children using profanity and discussing sex, drugs, and other topics that used to be reserved for adulthood.

To obtain an edge in the competitive game of life, as we've already seen, little boys and girls are urged to get a head start on their peers through advanced education. "Children of four are expected to act like six, with the result that they end up having the emotional needs of a child of two," notes Marian Blum, educational director of Wellesley College's Child Study Center.[7]

Divorce

Every year, there are more than 1.2 million divorces in the United States. Furthermore, according to various estimates, these divorces, along with countless marital separations, affect millions of children. These disruptions are a major cause of stress in a child's life and the source of a variety of health problems, including stomachaches and headaches.

Peer acceptance

One little second-grader was reduced to tears because her classmates made fun of her new hair style. Pressures from peers increase as a child gets older until they become a dominant force during the teenage years.

Death of a parent

As of 1982, more than 2.5 million children in the United States had lost at least one parent through death. By any psychosocial measurement of stress levels, the death of a loved one is a major candidate among the events that may cause health problems.

Moving to another home

Another major stress-causing event is a move. Yet almost 18 percent of American children move with their parents to a new home every year.

The parents of one fifth-grader brought the boy in for a checkup because he had been experiencing severe nausea many mornings just before school. As a result of his complaints, they had been keeping him home from school a day or so a week, and they were getting worried that he would fall far behind in his studies.

After examining him and having a talk with the parents, I determined that there was nothing physically wrong. But I did learn that the family had moved from one part of town to another. The boy was attending a new school where he had been forced to develop a completely new set of friends. He was under considerable stress as a consequence of the demands of his new surroundings—a fact that seemed clearly linked to his stomach problems.

After some counseling, the parents became more sensitive to their son's needs. Among other things, they helped him map out a strategy to make friends more quickly. He invited several of his new classmates for after-school play, outings to professional football and basketball games, and other get-togethers. Also, he got involved in the Boy Scouts, a favored group in his school, and he joined various sports teams. Soon, he actually became one of the most popular boys in the fifth grade, and his nausea disappeared.

Many other events in a child's life may lead to serious stress. These are just a few that various health professionals have emphasized as being of particular significance.

The Symptoms of Stress

Now, what are the symptoms of stress that may appear in a child? In other words, what illnesses or other disorders may signal the presence of too much pressure in a child's life? There are several possibilities.

Minor Illnesses

Various studies have shown that children with stress-related problems develop an unusual number of minor illnesses, particularly respiratory diseases and, as a complication, inflammations of the middle ear. This latter problem, known technically as otitis media, frequently follows or accompanies a cold, sore throat, or bronchitis.

A 1984 report by Dr. Barbara Starfield in the prestigious *New England Journal of Medicine* revealed that of the children with an average number of minor medical illnesses, more than two-thirds also had "psychosocial problems." In this context, "psychosocial problems" refers to psychological and social difficulties were often linked to stress. In contrast, less than a quarter of the children without these psychosocial problems had the minor medical illnesses.[8]

Serious Illnesses

In four other major studies, ranging from 1962 to 1982, a definite link was established between experiences of stress and various child health complaints. Specifically, these studies found that stress was accompanied by an increased incidence of streptococcal illnesses (severe bacterial infections), more injuries, longer-lasting illnesses, and longer hospital stays.

In commenting on these studies, one researcher has noted that "the mean duration of illnesses increased from 7 to about 10 days between children reporting low vs. high numbers of stressful events. . . . There is a striking consistency in the general pattern of these results, suggesting that highly stressed children are at greater risk for changes in health."[9]

There have also been suggestions in the medical literature that an association exists between stress and the exacerbation of illnesses such as asthma, diabetes, and hemophilia.[10]

Trips to the School Nurse

Children who are under stress tend to make more trips to see the school nurse, even though they do not have a serious illness. In one school, a policy was established to allow children aged five to twelve to leave the classroom without their teacher's permission for a visit to the school nurse. The researchers identified one subgroup of children, about 12 percent of all the students, who accounted for more than 50 percent of all visits to the nurse.

Who were these children?

There were more girls than boys. If they were under seven years old, they usually complained of a stomachache. If they were older than seven, they typically said they had a headache. Furthermore, their teachers reported that most of the youngsters were having academic or behavior problems, including difficulty in getting along with their peers. None had chronic medical disorders, however.[11]

Substance Abuse

Children under stress often turn to unhealthy and unproductive behavior, including substance abuse. The National Institute on Alcohol Abuse and Alcoholism has estimated that 1.3 million teenagers have serious drinking problems. Also, substance abuse is the leading cause of death among teenagers. Suicide and crime rates are up among adolescents, and excessive stress is a major contributor to these ills. Various researchers have also linked childhood stress to poor academic performance, high absenteeism, cigarette smoking, and dropping out of school.

Feeling Bad

Stress may cause a child to be overly tired, or to feel depressed, anxious, or otherwise out of sorts. Researchers Mary Ann and Charles Lewis of UCLA devised a "feel-bad" scale for children to try to determine what events in life created debilitating stress. They asked, "What happens that makes you feel bad, get upset, or nervous?"

The children's responses, which differed markedly from what many adults would consider stressful, highlighted the following sources of youthful stress: (1) events associated with a lack of self-esteem, such as "being the last one chosen on a team, or being left out of a group"; (2) strained parent-child relationships, such as a failure to spend enough time with parents or being restricted too much by family rules; and (3) "dislocations," including moving and changing schools. The researchers concluded that children with high "feel-bad" scores also were the most likely to feel sad, tired, worried, or negative about themselves.[12]

Numerous other studies have shown that a person's immune response—the ability of his body to ward off diseases—can be diminished by increased stress. Specifically, immune mechanisms may be affected by a weak sense of self, painful events like the death of a loved one, feelings of vulnerability, and mental illness. Studies of levels of antibodies, white blood cells, and other aspects of the body's chemistry have confirmed these conclusions.

In general, I've discovered in my practice that children who are under less pressure and who show fewer symptoms of stress are most likely to be resistant to various diseases. Also, their recovery time tends to be faster than those with heavy stress in their lives. Now, let's examine in more detail how your child can reduce stress levels and performance pressures.

Chapter Eight

Six Rules for Reducing a Child's Performance Pressures

One popular teenage girl was a classic example of the "jack of all trades and master of none." She was a class officer, a cheerleader, a participant on one of the school sports teams, and an extremely good student.

But she finally went too far in her personal commitments. She decided to assume the lead in one of her class plays *and* the chairmanship of a major dance *and* leadership in several other school projects. The result: She ran into some serious scheduling and coping problems.

The girl began to lapse into hysterics at the slightest provocation, and she started missing more and more classes because of an increased incidence of illness. After she had undergone a complete medical examination, it was apparent that she had developed a mild case of anemia and was the victim of excessive, chronic fatigue. Also, it seemed that she might be on the verge of developing some sort of problem with her immunological system.

Her doctor prescribed rest, a more appropriate diet, and certain stress–coping techniques to help her deal with the many pressures in her life. Among other things, he introduced her to a muscle-relaxation technique, which involved taking off about ten minutes in the middle of the day to sit quietly in an empty classroom. While she was there, she concentrated on tightening and then totally relaxing each of the major muscle groups in her body. She would begin with her feet and leg muscles and then move up through her entire body. Also, as she did this exercise, she spent time in prayer, asking God to take away her frustrations and release her from her anxieties.

Her physician encouraged her to eliminate several of her activities, including the latest ones she had taken on. Part of the challenge for the physician was convincing the girl that she really could be an adequate person without getting involved as a leader in so many different projects. When this fact finally sank in, she began to recover some of her former strength. Soon, the havoc, which stress had been wreaking on her body, subsided.

This particular case illustrates a number of different solutions to stress that I've found to be effective in dealing with "pressurized" young people. To explain in greater detail how these and other solutions to stress work, I've devised a set of "rules" for reducing performance pressure among children.

These rules, though they have certainly been effective for many of my patients, aren't meant to be an exhaustive, rigid list of what your child *must* do in order to reduce the stress in his or her life. Rather, they should be regarded as guidelines that will most likely be helpful to follow but can also be supplemented with other approaches as you see fit.

Rule #1: Assess the stress status of your child.

I always encourage the parents of my pediatric patients to ask themselves a series of probing key questions so that they can get a better idea of the pressures bearing down on their children. Some of the queries I suggest they answer about each youngster include the following:

▶ If I had to provide three words or terms that best describe my child, what would they be?
▶ What motivates my child?
▶ What are his main strengths, weaknesses, and interests?
▶ How does he relate to music? To sports? To academic work?
▶ Does his daily schedule allow him time to pursue activities that involve his strengths and interests?
▶ What does my child spend most of her day doing?
▶ Is my child overscheduled?

▶ What activity makes my child most happy?
▶ Does my child usually seem energetic? Fatigued?
▶ Is my child generous?
▶ Is she loving and affectionate? Does she need to be "stroked" or held often?

Next, I suggest that parents ask themselves several questions about their own attitudes, feelings, and involvements with each of their children. Here are some samples:

▶ How do I relate to my child's activities, interests, and inner motivations?
▶ How do I feel about my child's various traits and interests?
▶ To what extent am I involved in my child's life and daily schedule?

It's important for parents to ask themselves such questions in assessing their child's situation because good parents, by definition, aren't detached. They communicate, interact, and participate effectively with their children, verbally as well as by means of attitudes.

The key consideration here, though, is to interact or participate in a way that enhances or complements the natural talents and motivation of the child. In other words, it will be counterproductive for a parent to try to motivate a child to engage in an activity that the child dislikes intensely or in which the child has no natural ability. I've seen several cases, for instance, where a father would try to push and shove his son into a particular sport, but the boy hated the sport or had no natural aptitude for it or both.

I recall one father who had played competitive baseball as a boy. He assumed that his son should be at least as good, and probably better, at the sport than he had been. So he began to pitch balls to the boy at an early age, enrolled him in T-ball and Little League teams, and spent increasing numbers of hours training the youngster in the skills and lore of the sport.

The son had some natural ability as an athlete, but not as much as his father. Furthermore, he didn't like playing baseball nearly as much as he liked reading books. He wanted to please his dad, but he just couldn't live up to the parent's expectations. As a result, by the time he reached about ten or eleven years of age, the boy began to

beg his father to allow him to quit baseball and pursue other interests.

Fortunately, this father finally saw the light. Disappointed
though he was, he gave his son permission to quit baseball, and
eventually Dad learned to accommodate himself to the son's other
activities. It's just too bad that the father wasn't more tuned in at an
earlier point to his child's real interests and motivations. He had been
trying to fit a square peg into a round baseball hole, and the father-
son relationship was placed under a severe strain for a number of
years.

By the same token, there's not much point in trying to add additional parental pressure to a child who is already motivated. If you
go too far—if you try to build an even hotter "fire" under a child
who is already interested in a particular area—you may find yourself
undercutting the child's natural interest. It's like the supersalesman—
he knows when the pitch to the buyer has "taken," or when the sale
is made and the deal should be closed. The pursuit of a sale already
made will often produce the wrong outcome.

One father who was intensely interested in basketball and had
played a considerable amount when he was younger was overjoyed
to discover that his son was also interested in and talented at the
game. But by the time the son reached high school, the father had
become overinvolved in the activity. He tried to get the boy to practice his shots for hours on the weekends, when the youngster would
have preferred to be out playing golf or bowling with his buddies.
Also, the father, who had a flexible work schedule, showed up at
most of the son's practices in addition to all the games.

At first, this parent didn't take the hint when his son said, "Dad,
you know you don't have to come to *all* the practices. I wouldn't
mind if you skip a few."

But then, a friend, who had run into a similar problem with his
child, a girl who was an excellent gymnast, suggested that maybe
this father was overdoing it. "You know, I found that my daughter's
performance actually *improved* when I began to miss her practices.
I've even made it a point to skip some of the minor meets, and I think
that works to her advantage. She appreciates the independence. Kids
this age don't like to have a parent hovering around all the time."

So this basketball-father finally became convinced to try the
same approach. He skipped his son's practices and also missed occasional games. At first, he felt guilty about it.

"It was almost as though I wasn't supporting my son enough," he recalled.

But in fact, his son did just as well and sometimes did better than when the father had been around. Even more important, the boy cheerfully declared that it was perfectly all right with him if Dad couldn't make it to every game. He liked to have his parents there *most* of the time, but *every* time wasn't necessary at all!

I cite this case not to suggest that you use it as a formula for your involvement with your children. Rather, the experience illustrates how important it is for a parent to mesh his own interests and involvement with the interests and needs of the child. A thorough assessment of the child—and also of how the parent is relating and should be relating to the child—is an absolutely essential foundation for a stress-reduction strategy.

Rule #2: Don't try to live through your child.

An *absolute principle* for keeping pressure and stress on a child at healthy levels is that you can't expect a child to become exactly what you want him or her to be!

I know too many families where lives have been ruined or placed under undue strain because the mother or father wanted the child to be a doctor or a lawyer or something else. In many such cases, the *parent* originally wanted to go into the chosen field, but for some reason those ambitions may have been thwarted. The parent, unwilling to accept defeat, decides to try again through the child.

Typically, children in these situations revolt or underachieve. Or even if the child acquiesces and goes into the field that the parent has chosen, he will often change careers later and go into the occupation he really wants to pursue.

A professor from a major medical school whom I met on a plane trip was chatting with me about how children develop and mature. In the course of the conversation, he began to talk about how disappointed he was in his son, who had decided to pursue a rather unusual line of work.

"What do you suppose my son does?" he asked.

"I have no idea," I replied.

"He's a potter. He lives on the beach and has this little shop, but he barely makes ends meet. Frankly, I'm having a terrible time dealing with that. Here I am, a professor and a physician, respected in my field across the nation, and this boy has headed in the opposite direction."

But the more I talked with this man, the more I saw where his son's choice of professions came from. The father was a sensitive, artistic sort of person who liked the independent life. In fact, he expressed some dissatisfaction with having to work within the confines of a university community.

"I often think that someday, I'll set up my own practice and work for myself rather than an institution," he said.

"That's pretty much what your son is doing," I replied.

He didn't understand what I was talking about at first. But as we discussed the matter further, he began to see that his son had many of the same traits he did; the young man was just expressing those traits in different ways. For example, both father and son liked to be independent; both were artistically inclined (the father painted for a hobby); and both loved the seashore.

Unfortunately, the son had felt pressure and disapproval from the father during his teenage years, and he had rebelled. The father was a doctor who had wanted his son to be one, too, so that was exactly what the boy *wasn't* going to do! Consequently, the son expressed his native gifts and interests, which were similar to those of his father, but in a way that he could be himself.

If this father had backed off a little and put less pressure on his son to follow a predetermined career, the son might have drifted naturally in the father's direction. But given the nature of the father-son relationship that had developed, medicine just wasn't in the picture as a possible occupation for the son.

Another big mistake many parents these days make is to try to structure a child's life so as to put the child in a position to get a scholarship to a good college. Often, the parents themselves secretly wanted such a scholarship, but for some reason, they failed to get it when they were younger.

One father told me, "I've got to find a good sport for Michelle because that will give her an advantage in getting into a top-level college. Also, a top ranking in a sport will enable her to get some scholarship money from a college, and I won't have to pay for her education. That could save me thousands and thousands of dollars!"

Fortunately, his little girl did turn out to be good at sports, and she enjoyed her father's participation in athletic activities with her.

Also, as she got older, her father relaxed more in his ambitions for her, in part because it became evident that she really would be an excellent tennis and basketball player.

But in many cases, the parent gets too involved. Mom or Dad either tries to exert too much control over the child's academic or career direction or begins to live through the child, and that will usually result in tremendous frustration and unhappiness when the youngster fails to live up to expectations.

Rule #3: Avoid parental pushiness—at practically any cost!

In some ways, this rule is a corollary of Rule #2. A parent who wants to live through his child will usually end up pushing the youngster too much. But pushiness may also manifest itself in various other forms in parents who are pressuring their children to excel. Two particularly vivid examples illustrate this parental tendency.

The math whiz.

One ten-year-old child I know was very good at math. But her natural talents began to be obscured and her performance level deteriorated because her parents were always putting her on the spot.

When she failed to do a quick calculation in her head, her mother or father might say, "What's wrong? You're supposed to be good at math! Don't take so long to come up with an answer."

The more they pushed, however, the more the girl froze up. Her mind just wouldn't work nimbly with someone standing over her, telling her that she had to perform or that she wasn't performing up to par.

"I don't know all the answers all the time," she would reply. Or "I can't think when you're pressing me like this."

But the parents didn't get the message—at least, not until the youngster started making lower grades in math. Also, she began to be sick on the days that her teacher scheduled math tests.

The parents finally brought her to see me, and I soon found that she was extremely angry about the pressure being put on her. As I talked with her alone, she said, "I can't do what they want me to do! They expect me to do better than I'm capable of doing. They say I'm smart, but I don't think I'm so smart! I've really been doing badly on those tests, and I don't even like school any more!"

In fact, this girl had a very high aptitude in math. But her parents had expected too much of her at a young age. They had demanded a higher performance level than she was capable of, emotionally or developmentally.

So I laid out the problem for the parents. Then, I suggested that they stop pressuring the girl.

"For the time being, I think you have to eliminate all pressure on her," I said. "Don't expect anything. Let her know you love her and accept her, no matter how well she does. And *mean* it when you say it!"

The father at first resisted: "Look, we know she's gifted. She should be doing better than the other kids!"

"Put yourself in her shoes," I said. "Take one of the questions you're asking her and imagine someone putting the same multiplication or division problem to *you*. Picture the teacher or parent or other authority figure standing over you and pushing you to give an immediate answer. What's 15 times 17? What's 12 times 19? Quick, what is it? Hurry!"

The father—who might have become angry at this point and stamped out of the room—began to smile. "Okay, okay, I get the point," he said.

It wasn't easy for the parents to stop pushing their daughter to achieve. But as I pointed out to them, they had nothing to lose. She was underachieving, and her performance level had been on a steady decline. Doing anything differently, including following my suggestion, seemed better than maintaining the status quo. They backed off entirely, and the girl's performance level improved almost immediately.

As I said, though, it hasn't been easy for the mother and father. They sometimes find themselves falling back into the pushy pattern that had resulted in all their daughter's academic and emotional problems. But they're trying, and in general, they're making significant progress in replacing old bad habits with better ones.

The sick baseball player.

One small boy told me, "I don't like to go to Little League practice because I'm no good at baseball. The coaches and parents expect me to stand up there and swing at fast balls, and I can never hit them.

I'm afraid those pitchers are going to hit me. They have hit other kids! But everybody looks at me, and a lot of them laugh, and some guy's always yelling, 'Why aren't you swinging?' But I just can't do it right!"

This youngster had been having an increased incidence of stomachaches and headaches, which usually occurred when he was scheduled for a baseball game or practice. He dreaded the games, and his reaction was understandable, given the pattern of his experience at the plate. In addition to the other abuse and pressure he had to endure, he told me that when it was his turn to bat, the other children on the team would say, "Aw, don't put him up to bat! We're going to lose if you do!"

Also, at school he was always the last to be chosen for a sports team during gym class. He seemed to have no aptitude or interest in athletics, yet his parents insisted that he play and participate. As a result, he had become extremely anxious and had begun to have physical symptoms, such as a frequently upset stomach, stomachaches, and headaches.

I told his parents that they had to be more sensitive to their child's interests and talents. "If he doesn't like baseball, he shouldn't be playing it," I told them. "Furthermore—and this is especially true if he's not good at the sport—his wishes should be respected if he wants to give it up. There's no point in trying to force a child to do something he can't do. And if you do try to force it, you'll pay the price in terms of his health and your relationship with him."

There's a fine line between being involved and supportive and being pushy like these two sets of parents. You can usually tell that you've crossed the line if your child becomes unhappy, anxious, or irritable, or if she begins to have stress-related emotional or physical symptoms. But there's no reason to reach this point if you operate within a low-stress environment such as we'll discuss next in Rule #4.

Rule #4: Create a low-stress environment for your child.

It's quite possible to emphasize high achievement and excellence, yet at the same time maintain a happy, low-stress milieu for your child to develop properly. Here are some suggestions that should help you "depressurize" your home and family.

Participate.

Parents who send their children to wonderful private schools, camps, or special academic or sports programs—but who don't get involved very much themselves—will almost always be disappointed, or at least disconcerted, by the way their youngsters turn out. On the other hand, those who play catch in the back yard or shoot baskets at the local playground or help when necessary with homework will usually see significant dividends in their children's performance levels.

But a word of caution: Participation must not turn into pushiness or trying to live through your child. At this point, refer back to Rules #2 and #3. The suggestions there must be balanced against this need to participate.

Be supportive.

Children must always sense that their parents are behind them; they must believe Mom and Dad are on their team. I've seen many parents undercut their own stated purposes as they say they want their child to excel, yet at the same time, they levy devastating criticism and ridicule on the child when he falls short.

On the other hand, false reassurance is worse than ridicule. The children must know you love, respect, understand, and accept them as they are. Who among us is without blame or fault?

A child must be able to fail and know that he's still loved and accepted by his parents. Otherwise, he'll most likely develop serious insecurities and will end up lacking the confidence necessary to perform at his maximum potential.

Provide opportunities and suggestions, but don't try to control.

This guideline is perhaps the most difficult for active, participating parents to follow with their children. Too often, a mother or father will provide various opportunities, such as good schooling, expensive computers, a wide array of sports equipment, or whatever.

But then, the parent will make it clear that strings are attached by saying: "I send you to that expensive school because I expect you to use your education to get ahead in life! But you're consistently coming in with these bad grades!" "That computer is intended to be used for your school science projects, not just for fooling around and wasting your time like some electronic hacker!" or "What did I give you that baseball gear for? You never use it!"

This sort of outburst from a parent *never does any good at all*. In fact, you can be fairly certain that this approach will do more harm than good. Parents who rely on this *modus operandi* are trying desperately to control their children; they usually already realize that control is out of their hands.

All any parent can really do is to provide opportunities for a child and perhaps a few suggestions about how the youngster might use those opportunities. But a parent must be willing to have those opportunities ignored by the child or used in ways the parent wasn't expecting.

I recognize, however, that it's hard to assume such an attitude. For moms and dad who have paid out a lot of money for various types of toys or equipment, it can be frustrating to see those gifts go completely unused. But that's part of the monetary risk we must take as parents. Sometimes, the baseball bats and gloves we buy will launch a successful amateur or professional career. But many times, they won't; they just give temporary pleasure or fond remembrances.

An even more frustrating situation may be one involving a parent who invests a great deal of time in a particular interest for a child, only to find the child heading in a completely different direction as he or she gets older.

I remember one mother who gave her little daughter dance and gymnastic lessons when the girl was still a preschooler. The mother carted the girl back and forth to lessons on trips that covered thousands of miles over the years. Also, she took her to various meets and many, many recitals. Her goal: that the girl either would make the Olympics as a gymnast or would be admitted to a major ballet company.

"I was sure that we'd at least come close to *one* of those goals," she said.

However, by the time the girl reached age ten, it was obvious the mother was going to be disappointed. The youngster wasn't winning or even placing at any of the gymnastic meets, and she was only a mediocre dancer. Even more important, the girl *hated* these disciplines, and she kept begging her mother to let her stop.

"I don't have any time to be with my friends," she said. "I just want some time to play with them or be alone."

Finally, this mother did give up when the girl suffered a couple of injuries from the activities. This parent felt thoroughly defeated and discouraged. But I reminded her, "You know, you can give your child an opportunity, but you can't control the future. You can't determine ahead of time exactly what her life is going to be like."

"But I've wasted so much time!" she said.

"No, you haven't!" I replied. "I know you're disappointed. But I also know that you have a good relationship with your daughter. She loves you, and she doesn't want to hurt you. But she's reached the end of her rope with these activities. These latest injuries have pushed her over the edge, and I'm afraid that the good relationship you have may sour if you continue to push her.

"Even if you stop the gymnastics and dancing, think of what you've given her. She's had a lot of time to develop a close relationship with you. She's developed her muscles and bones in ways that give her a good foundation for a healthy life. And who knows? She's athletic and may very well find another sport or activity that will allow her to use her strength and conditioning."

I noted that she had disciplined herself, a quality that would help her in dealing with life's other challenges. Also, she had developed a sense of what she wanted to do and what she didn't want to do.

This mother decided to relinquish the close control she had been exerting over her daughter and let the future unfold at a more relaxed, natural pace. Right now, I don't know how or if the girl will use the skills she learned when she was younger. But I do know that she and her mother are on the right track in their interactions.

Rule #5: Fine-tune your emphasis on excelling and winning.

When the late pro football coach Vince Lombardi said, "Winning isn't everything—it's the only thing," he might have had many contemporary parents in mind. Talk to any parent of a child these days, and there's almost a 100 percent certainty that you can uncover some horror story about an overemphasis on winning and achieving, whether in the academic or the athletic fields.

In just the last few weeks, I've heard countless such stories, including fights among parents at junior tennis matches, backstabbing at parent-teacher meetings because of a child's failure to make the top grade on a science competition, and outrage at the failure of an aspiring thespian to be given the lead in a class play.

Distorted views of winning and excelling frequently arise from three insidious forces: (1) a childhood version of cutthroat competition; (2) a prevalent tendency toward performance anxiety; and (3) a destructive form of perfectionism.

1. The question of competition.

Let me say at the outset that I'm *not* of the school of thought recommending that competition be outlawed. For example, I'm not for eliminating the possibility of winning at games, abandoning awards for individual achievement, or getting rid of grades for academic excellence. Some child development specialists have suggested that winning be eliminated from play. But I don't see that as possible or even desirable for most children, especially as they get older. The typical youngster I know *likes* competition. He's stimulated by the idea that somebody may come in first, second, or third—that somebody may win a prize—and that *he* may be the winner.

Furthermore, winning—or at least trying very hard so that you do as well as possible and improve your performance to some degree—can build confidence. I'm reminded of one situation where an intramural youth soccer team lost every game. The members of the team lost heart, and soon, few were showing up for the games. But at the end of the season, the coach did a very wise thing. He called all the members of the team and gave them this advice: "I know we lost all our games this season, but I don't want you to give up. You have ability, and I think on a different team, you might have won some games. You might even have won the championship. The main problem with the team was probably my coaching, but in any event, you shouldn't blame yourself. Just be sure to try again next year, okay?"

As a result of this encouragement, most of the members of the team *did* try again, and several were on teams that were championship contenders. Before long, their confidence in themselves and in their ability at the sport returned. So it's important to emphasize the *long haul* for children who experience early losses or failures.

Doing poorly on a sports team or on a few math tests or in some other endeavor doesn't necessarily set the tone for your entire life. Children in these situations should be provided with a broader perspective on achievement, a perspective that reaches beyond one game, test, event, or season. They should also be advised and instructed about how to do better next time. Then, the parent or other adult talking to them should encourage them to try again. This way, one series of losses won't promote an ongoing "loser's mentality."

2. The plague of performance anxiety.

Too often, by placing an undue emphasis on winning or high achievement, a parent helps create anxiety in the child that inhibits performance. I'm familiar with a number of cases of test anxiety, for example, where a child may exhibit above-average intelligence and skills in daily work, but then do miserably on a test.

Sometimes, this poor performance becomes evident when exams are administered at school, with the result that the youngster ends up with bad grades and a poor grade point average. Other times, a child may learn to do well at school, but then "freezes up" on national academic tests, such as the Scholastic Aptitude Test (SAT).

In most cases, the anxiety that produces this poor performance arises from the child's belief or assumption that a test is of extreme, overriding importance. In a sense, he begins to think that his whole life and future depend on it, and he becomes immobilized. He can't think clearly or quickly, and the more difficulty he encounters when he first starts on a particular test, the more paralyzed he becomes. Low scores and a poor academic standing are the results.

In one situation, a high-school student typically did quite well on his tests at school, and his academic ranking was near the top of his class. But when it came to the standard national tests, such as the SAT, he flopped. When he walked into the huge testing center, he would find himself confronted by strange test supervisors, strange testing sheets, and an entirely strange environment.

His first reaction was, "I don't like this place. I don't feel comfortable here." Also, after a couple of bad performances on these tests, he developed a pattern or habit of failure. He *expected* not to do very well, and sure enough, he didn't!

A counselor the boy consulted about this problem had some wise, helpful suggestions. She traced the main source of the anxiety back to an assumption that the boy was making—and that his parents and friends reinforced—that these national tests were going to be the absolute determinant of his future. The message he was getting: He *had* to do well on them, or he could expect *not* to get into a good college, *not* to be in a position to attend a good graduate school and, finally, *not* to succeed in life.

But then, the counselor pointed out the fallacies in the assumption. First of all, she laid out a worst case scenario—that the boy might not improve at all on these tests—and she demonstrated that this result might not be all that bad.

The counselor noted, for instance, that many people have become resounding successes without attending college at all. Furthermore, many who have done poorly on their grades (which was not the case with this student) have ended up running major corporations and even countries. Finally, even if the boy performed below his potential on the standard national tests, the counselor assured him that his academic record would still put him in a strong position to attend a good college.

But that was the worst case. There was still a very good chance that a much better scenario would unfold. "I'm convinced you can improve your performance on these tests," the counselor said. "All you have to do is formulate a strategy that will help you do better."

The first part of the strategy was to recognize that the standard tests weren't all-important. To reinforce this view, the counselor told the parents that they needed to help by de-emphasizing the importance of the tests.

"You should first decide that you can live with whatever score your son achieves," she said. "Sure, you want him to do as well as possible. But believe me, what I told him about the importance of these tests really is true. They don't represent all of life. Your boy may do horrendously on the SAT and still be a big success in business or whatever. Yet you yourselves have to accept that fact and believe it and communicate it to your son. The more he becomes convinced that you'll accept him, regardless of his performance, the better he'll tend to do."

This approach wasn't easy for the mother and father because both of them had excelled in school, and they put a high premium on academic performance and admission to a top-level college. But they agreed in principle with the counselor, and they resolved to do all they could to ease the tension around the home as the day for the exams approached.

But that was just the first step. In the second place, the student needed to learn to deal more effectively with his anxiety.

"In part, you're failing to perform up to par because you're letting the pressure of a strange situation get to you," his counselor said. "One solution to this is to get more familiar with the testing procedures and with the test facility. That will help you become more relaxed."

The student, under the counselor's guidance, did some research into how the standard national aptitude and achievement tests were formulated and graded. He also took a short course in techniques for mastering the tests. In addition, he went to the site of the next scheduled test and looked over the physical surroundings, imagining himself sitting at one of the tables with an exam booklet.

By thus familiarizing himself with the test procedures, the probable categories of questions, and the physical setup for the exam—and by accepting the fact that the test wasn't going to make or break his future success in life—the boy found he was able to relax more.

So when the day for the next exam rolled around, the student was keyed up, as were all his classmates, but his natural concern and anticipation didn't degenerate into debilitating performance anxiety. As he walked into the testing facility this time, his attitude was different. He knew what to expect and how to take the test most effectively, and he performed much better.

3. Perfectionism and paralysis.

A variation on the theme of becoming immobilized by the pressure to perform well is what I call "paralysis through perfectionism." This problem can emerge in any number of different fields, from academics to sports.

One classic case is the writer's block. Some young people are brought up to think that they have to get everything exactly correct in essays or themes they write. Their penmanship has to be perfect. Their grammar has to be perfect. Their syntax has to be perfect. Their organization and style have to be perfect. Moreover, if anything *isn't* perfect, they believe they should stop moving forward and work on the difficulty in question until it's been corrected.

Of course, there's an inherent, fatal flaw with this approach to writing. *Nobody* is perfect, not even the greatest author. There's always something that's not quite right, something that can be improved. So if the average writer keeps stopping to correct and improve things until he achieves perfection, he'll eventually come to a complete standstill. He'll be paralyzed by his perfectionism.

Here's a related illustration of how a similar difficulty developed with a young tennis player. A racquet was placed in this boy's hand when he was about six, but his father didn't emphasize the joy of running and hitting. Rather, he stressed how essential it was for the youngster to do everything right: "Your grip *must* look like this. Your forehand *must* move like this. Your footwork *must* go like this."

Eventually, the child began to focus not on developing a natural athletic style and on enjoying himself, but on doing all his motions and movements just right. By the time the boy had turned eight, he was a nervous wreck on the court. You could see the tension and anxiety in the contorted features of his face. In a typical one-hour practice session, he would dissolve into tears two or three times. Also, he easily became confused when he was told to follow a different pattern or try a different drill from what his father had taught him, and with his confusion came more tears.

At this point, I don't know where this boy's tennis game is going. But I do know that when he becomes an adult, he will have to pick up a lot of emotional pieces to put his life together.

As it stands now, he can perform reasonably well on the court for an eight-year-old. But his thinking is mechanistic, and he appears to lack the freedom, creativity, and interest necessary to enjoy the game. He plays and performs only because his father wants him to and only according to his father's predetermined patterns. In a sense, even though this boy is capable of moving about, from one side of the court to the other, he can't play consistently without his father's presence and direction. He represents a form of partial paralysis through perfectionism.

Rule #6: Teach your child proven "tricks" and techniques for reducing stress.

Many special techniques have emerged in the last couple of decades for reducing stress, and many of them are applicable to children as well as to adults.

For example, various forms of distraction may help to eliminate the pressure a young child feels in certain situations. I regularly see children who exhibit extreme symptoms of stress, including emotional upsets, when they have sustained an injury or are about to get an injection. Yet by using certain relaxation techniques, I find I can avoid using anesthesia on the young patients.

One eight-year-old boy came in with a cut on his arm. Obviously, his arm was hurting, but he was also quite afraid of what I was going to do to stop the pain. So I immediately got his attention by asking, "What is the most wonderful thing that you think you would like to do—if you could choose anything in the world?"

The boy said, "I'd like to go to a beach in Bermuda, where we went last month."

"Okay, now I want you to close your eyes and think about that beach," I said. "Make a picture of it in your mind, and imagine you're there in slow motion. See yourself playing on that beach and going swimming in the water. But do it very slowly. And think about the best part of that beach. Is it the sand? Or the warm air? Or the saltwater? How about the shells?"

As I talked, I also began to work on the boy's arm, putting on antiseptic, administering a local anesthetic, and then sewing up the laceration. My work was finished before he was really aware of what was happening. In effect, he had succeeded in lowering his stress levels, including his anticipation of the pain he thought he was going to experience.

I've found other techniques to be helpful, and I've often recommended them to parents. For example, if a child looks as though she wants to scream out of frustration, fear, or some other emotion, encouraging her to scream can be beneficial. Many times, just getting the approval from an authority figure to "let it all out" can provide a significant calming influence.

(Of course, in some circumstances this approach may backfire. If a child seems to be getting into the habit of throwing tantrums or abusing parents with angry outbursts, it's important to let the child know that such patterns of behavior aren't acceptable or respectful. But in some circumstances, the freedom to express intense emotions may be appropriate and helpful. You'll probably have to experiment in different circumstances to see what works with your child and what doesn't.)

Another technique involves telling the child to focus on his favorite sport and imagine that he's playing in an exciting game or match. One parent of a baseball enthusiast suggested this scenario when his son seemed depressed about an unpleasant encounter with classmates at school: "You're in the bottom of the ninth, the score is tied, the bases are loaded, and you come up to bat with two outs. Orel Hershiser [star pitcher for the Los Angeles Dodgers] is on the mound. What happens?"

The boy began to paint a dramatic mental picture of how he stood up to the pitcher and managed to get a base hit and drive in the winning run. By the time he had finished this imaginary game, his worries about school had dissipated, and he was ready to move on to his homework.

Getting older children who are under stress to become more "tuned in" to their feelings and to express them openly is an effective approach. For example, I may say, "Pay very close attention to how you're feeling toward your parents and schoolmates. What's the main way you feel today?"

Usually, the initial response will be "unhappy" or "uncomfortable" or "bored." But when we continue to talk, and the child becomes more comfortable opening up to me and delving more deeply into his feelings, I'll often get an admission that anger is involved. When a youngster sees the real driving force in his emotions, he's better able to deal with it. Just putting that anger on the table so that he and I can look at it, discuss it, and analyze it is enough to rob the feeling of much of its power. When the power of a feeling such as anger decreases, so does the level of stress that it's producing.

Encouraging older children to go off by themselves to a quiet place is still another technique. I'll say, "Try to find a quiet place in your mind." They might imagine themselves walking in some peaceful woods or standing by a stream or viewing a breathtaking vista of a mountain range. "For about ten minutes, just think about the surroundings that you imagine you're in," I'll add. Typically, by the time they emerge from this reverie, the pressures they were feeling have disappeared.

Dr. Herbert Benson of the Harvard Medical School has written extensively on the elicitation of the "relaxation response" as a means to manage stress. In his books, including *The Maximum Mind,* he suggests a classic relaxation technique that I've modified as follows:

1. Pick a "focus word" or phrase that is central to your belief

system. For example, a Christian or Jew might pick a biblical phrase like "God is love."

2. Next, twice a day, for ten to twenty minutes at a time, sit down in a quiet place and close your eyes.

3. Begin to breathe regularly, and concentrate on your breathing.

4. As you breathe out, say your focus word or phrase to yourself and concentrate exclusively on the word or phrase.

5. When outside thoughts intrude—and you can be sure they will—gently turn away from them and go back to saying your focus phrase or word.

This technique has proved to be effective for adults in lowering high blood pressure and reducing stress-related disorders, such as headaches, stomachaches, and backaches. And I believe the same can be said for some children, especially older ones.

Obviously, it's not so easy to get a rambunctious elementary school child to sit still for ten minutes and focus on a Bible verse. But if you can turn this experience into a game, you may find a more positive response and a means to reduce stress levels.

For example, one mother of a highly stressed nine-year-old daughter, who was experiencing regular stomachaches, said, "I'll bet I can close my eyes and say 'Jesus loves me' to myself longer than you can."

The little girl lasted about one minute the first time. But then, her mother hit on the idea of awarding a "prize" to the person who could go the longest, the prize being a flashy bead that could be added to one of the girl's favorite necklaces. This time, she made it for about four minutes, and in later sessions, she managed to go even longer. Furthermore, introducing the girl to the quieting-down experience did wonders for reducing her gastrointestinal symptoms of stress.

In general, though, the more formal stress-reduction techniques work best for older children and adults. Very young children typically need approaches that either divert them or tie into their sense of play.

Now, let's turn to a related topic—the problem of too much pressure to perform in sports and exercise. I've already touched on some aspects of this subject, but more detail is needed about the medical dimensions and dangers that are involved.

Chapter Nine

Can Kids Overdose on Sports or Exercise?

Parents these days are receiving conflicting messages about fitness and athletics for their children.

On the one hand, they have heard the surgeon general declare, "The fitness of our youth is a national tragedy." They have also been told—by no less an authority than the President's Council on Physical Fitness and Sports—that the physical fitness level of public school children, aged six to seventeen, showed no improvement from 1975 to 1985. Furthermore, the council charged, tests used to measure fitness levels reveal that "the percentage of youth performing progressively worse is alarming."

At the same time that fitness is down, sports injuries seem to be up. In fact, children are suffering a veritable explosion of sports injuries, including stress fractures in the legs, "Little League elbow," and swimmer's shoulder, according to Dr. Lyle J. Micheli, an assistant clinical professor at the Harvard Medical School and chief of sports medicine at Children's Hospital in Boston.

Dr. Micheli brings these two trends—low fitness and high sports injury rates—together in this way: "Overall fitness is down, so that if children do an intensive athletic activity for an hour five times a week, it's a setup for injury."[1]

Too Much Pressure to Perform in Sports—Too Little Attention to Basic Fitness and Safety

I've encountered numerous instances of children who have been the targets of so much pressure to perform in sports that they've gone too far. They've pushed their bodies up to and beyond safe limits, and serious injuries have resulted. I've included a few of these cases here.

The superathletic ten-year-old.

One boy was well on his way to becoming a superathlete by the time he was ten. He excelled, regardless of the sport. Yet his father wanted more. He felt his son had the capability of reaching the top in one or more sports, and that meant either rising to Olympic level achievements or making a professional team. So this father demanded that the boy run every day, go through a calisthenic and weight-lifting routine four days a week, and in general live a Spartan existence, devoted to the single goal of athletic excellence.

Unfortunately, the regimen turned out to be too rigorous. The boy started reacting to the pressure, both physically and emotionally.

In particular, he suffered several twisted ankles and wrist strains. In addition, while training for a track meet, he first strained a muscle and then tore some ligaments. These physical problems, along with the relentless pressure he felt from his father to perform, caused the boy to be overwhelmed with fatigue and a sense of being burned out.

This father had failed to realize that young bodies, which are still undergoing bone and muscle growth, are vulnerable to injury from overuse. He had assumed that the more training and exercise his son did, the stronger he would become and the better athlete he would be. But in fact, the training passed a safe threshold, and the boy's body began to break down.

At the same time—as his injuries multiplied and he engaged in high-pressure, serious sports involvement rather than youthful play—he reacted emotionally. Children of ten are just beginning to reach the age when they can concentrate in a fairly mature fashion on the demands of a sport. But the process of specializing and pushing the body and mind to its limits has to be regulated carefully.

Increasingly, experts in the field of child athletic development are cautioning that if a child peaks too early, physically or emotionally, in his sport, he'll never reach his full potential. For example, there's a movement among leaders in junior tennis, including former professional stars Stan Smith and Arthur Ashe, to de-emphasize high-pressure competition, early specialization, and national rankings in the ten- to twelve-year age group. Rather, they advocate that the younger players develop a well-rounded fitness and athletic program. Then, they can specialize and move toward a tennis-playing peak when they get older.

To be sure, these junior tennis experts recognize the importance of ongoing, regular tennis development at early ages. But they point out that most great players didn't reach their emotional and physical peaks until at least their late teens. This approach is firmly rooted in what we understand now about the physiological and emotional needs of preadolescent and early adolescent youths.

The father in my illustration finally acknowledged that his son was confronting some serious physical and emotional problems and that these concerns had to be resolved before he could resume pressing ahead toward his sports objectives. But the boy had been so discouraged by his injuries and his mental fatigue that he didn't even want to think about sports for a while. The youngster's attitude frustrated the father, but he realized he had no choice but to be patient and wait for his son to show further interest. Otherwise, he would be courting serious and perhaps permanent damage to his son.

About a year later, the youngster did begin to show some interest in returning to sports. Although he lacked the interest he had displayed when he was younger, he still went on to become a fairly good amateur athlete. But he probably achieved well below his potential because of the unfortunate early pressure to perform.

The would-be football player

Another boy aspired from an early age to become a superior football player. So to increase his muscle power and bulk, he began to lift weights seriously, beginning at about age twelve. His exercise program consisted of an hour or more of heavy lifting, three to four times a week.

As in the previous situation involving the ten-year-old, this older boy was still growing, and the heavy exercise damaged his developing bones. Specifically, he developed a serious problem in his back—an injured disc—which produced agonizing pain and required long periods of rest. Needless to say, this health problem interrupted his football career. He was able to play sporadically on his high-school team, but the pain from the back injury recurred several times, and he was forced to miss games and practices so that his body could recover and heal.

In fact, the best thing this boy could have done would have been

to stop playing football altogether. But he refused to give up his athletic ambitions, and his parents, who were avid football fans, ration-
alized that he would "grow out of" the injury. But he never did, and
he finally had to drop out of football at the end of high school.

The "Little League elbow"

A third boy, who was eleven, complained about severe pains in
his right elbow and shoulder. He had just pitched six innings for his
junior boys' baseball team, and he could hardly move his arm.

On examining him, I discovered that he had a classic case of
"Little League elbow," an overuse injury that typically afflicts young
pitchers. His bones and muscles were still growing and developing,
and he had gone too far in this particular game. He had pushed himself physically beyond the capabilities of his age level. (We'll discuss
this injury in more detail in a later section.)

Fortunately, this was the first time that the boy had experienced
this sort of pain, and I suspected that rest would restore his arm completely. The mistake he had made was to try to "pitch through the
pain" that he had started feeling around the third inning. He should
have stopped at the first twinge. But he had a no-hitter going; his
team was in contention for the play-offs; and he was determined to
do everything he could to win.

At the end of the examination, I warned, "You mustn't do any
more pitching or similar exercise with this arm until the pain is gone
completely—*and* until I give you the go-ahead after another
checkup. If you go back too soon, you may very well sustain a permanent injury."

Reluctantly, he agreed with my recommendation, and his parents concurred. As it happened, the injury required him to sit out for
the rest of the season. But his arm *did* heal, and he was able to return
to pitch the next season.

This time, though, he was more prudent. He *and* his parents
acknowledged that he wasn't an adult and he couldn't perform at
adult levels. He was still a growing boy, and he had to keep that fact
in mind, regardless of any pressure he felt from his coaches, from his
teammates, or from inside himself. So he determined to play *only*
within safe limits and to stop immediately upon experiencing any
pain or undue fatigue.

These practical situations should give you a general idea of some of the dangers that may arise when children get overinvolved in exercise or athletics. But now, let's take a closer look at the injuries that may accompany the wrong emphasis on sports and consider what you can do about them.

Kids Who Have Too Much Sports Activity: A Guide to Identifying and Preventing Athletic Injuries

Injuries are inevitable when your child gets involved in sports. The answer to this problem, however, is *not* to avoid sports or become so afraid of what may happen that both you and your child lose the joy of participation and competition. Athletic activity and physical fitness are essential components for the health of any child, and it's important for a youngster to be involved regularly in some physical endeavor. So rather than stay away from athletics, the best approach to a sport is, first, to know what the dangers are and, second, to develop a sound plan to minimize or prevent them.

In general, there are three major ways for a child to prevent sports injuries: (1) avoid overuse of the body in playing a sport; (2) become as fit as possible, so that muscle and bone structures can withstand the physical demands of the activity; and (3) avoid contact sports with others more mature than he or she is.

I want to introduce you first to some of the major dangers and health hazards associated with various sports and activities. Also, we'll consider some general guidelines to help a child avoid overuse of his or her body during the period of growth. Now, here are some key health problems in children that are often linked to athletic activity—and some suggestions about how to prevent them.

Fatigue, strains, or pains after intense workouts at a sports camp

Typically, these injuries and discomforts result from going abruptly from a relaxed, sedentary pace to high-intensity training. A child may exercise vigorously only a few hours a week and then plunge into four- to eight-hour-a-day workouts at a camp. In such situations, soreness and injuries can be expected to occur.

The solution: Don't necessarily keep your child out of a camp. Just check the camp thoroughly to be sure that the intensity of the activity isn't too much for a child at your youngster's stage of development. Determine such things as how children are grouped; who is the sports consultant; and how the camp is regarded by other adults.

In general, I'd say that any camp that has intense workouts of more than three or four hours a day for children under twelve is going too far. In most cases, vigorous activity of more than five hours a day is too much for any growing child (and for that matter, it may be too much for most professional athletes!).

It's a good idea to start your child on a more planned, structured physical fitness program before the formal training begins at the sports camp. Strength and flexibility exercises are especially helpful. A typical sound fitness program might encompass a round of bent-leg situps, pushups, chinups, and flexibility exercises, such as toe touching. Regular runs, including longer distances of about a mile, two to three times a week, and also periodic sprinting can be good preparation as well.

But avoid exercises during hot, humid weather. Also, have him drink plenty of fluids; allow him to rest or walk part of the time. In addition, the course should be flat and easy to follow. With such preliminary training, the youngster will be in better shape and less likely to sustain an injury.

Growth-related physical problems

As a child grows, bone growth and other changes that occur in various parts of the body may make a child more vulnerable to athletic injuries. For example, as the skeletal structure grows and expands, muscles and tendons may not keep up with the bone. Consequently, a child may develop tight hamstrings (the msucles in the back of the thigh) and Achilles' tendons (the ropelike tendon at the back of the heel). Unless careful attention is paid to exercises that promote flexibility, sudden movements on the athletic field may cause injuries to these parts of the body.

Also, there's sometimes a tendency during childhood growth for the spine to arch. This condition, called "lordosis," may be the source of back pain or stress fractures, including fractures of the discs in the spine. Obviously, vigorous athletic activity may place a child with this condition even more at risk. In addition, hips that become tipped forward as a result of this condition may make it hard for a youngster to participate effectively in sports like soccer or activities like dancing. Stretching exercises can help this condition; see your doctor for suggestions.

Another problem with the youthful skeleton may involve the growth of the legs at different rates. Obviously, if one leg is longer than the other, the child is going to have trouble playing many sports effectively.[2]

If your child has these or similar complaints or traits, you should see your physician and get advice about the type of sport and level of activity that is appropriate.

In general, any abnormalities that occur as part of the growth process call for an immediate evaluation of a child's athletic activity. Exercising too hard or too long on bones that are not aligned properly or are growing in unusual directions will only increase the risk of serious injury. On the other hand, your physician may be able to suggest remedial exercises or devices that will help to correct the condition and hasten the time when your son or daughter can engage safely in some form of athletics.

Finally, every parent of *every* growing child should remember this: The expanding, growing parts of the bones in a child—especially the relatively soft "growth plates" (epiphysis) at the ends of the growing bones—are more vulnerable to injury than the mature, hardened bones of the adult. So as you guide your child in her sports activity, don't overdo it! Encourage physical activity and solid fitness, but watch for signs of fatigue and complaints of pain.

It's probably best for a preadolescent child to avoid weight training. Such exercises may cause damage to the epiphysis. Instead of using barbells or similar devices, it's best for very young children to concentrate on keeping fit by doing exercises that involve moving and raising their bodies, such as pushups, chinups, bent-leg situps, and the like.

Above all, don't encourage the child to perform at top *adult* levels of intensity. Certainly, most children are capable of performing at endurance levels above those of many adults. But their bones and other body parts are more vulnerable. In practical terms, a one- or two-mile run is fine for most children, and this distance can be covered by most youngsters as often as three or four times a week. But daily five-mile jogs and marathons are out!

The important thing is to strike a balance between the extremes. Your child should maintain an adequate level of activity to stay at a top level of fitness, but not go so far that injury results to the youthful physique.

Injuries from poor equipment, playing conditions, or facilities

A common complaint I hear from children is, "My feet hurt when I run!"

The usual reason is that shoes are too small or don't fit properly. The obvious answer is to get new shoes that *do* fit properly! Choose *all* athletic equipment with great care. Also, if protective baseball or football headgear doesn't fit, contact with another player or with the ball is more likely to produce an injury.

According to a study by the U.S. Consumer Products Safety Commission, child athletes at age four or younger most commonly sustain injuries to the face or head. Those from five to fourteen suffer arm injuries more than any other. And children fifteen and older are treated most often for ankle and knee injuries (often as a consequence of participation in contact sports like football).

Many of these injuries could be prevented if children wore adequate, properly fitted equipment. For example, Little League players now wear a hard helmet when they bat, but they should also have on an optional protective face mask. These devices are provided by most teams, but few players use them. With these face masks, many of the injuries caused by wild pitches to the face could be prevented.

"Little League elbow" and swimmer's shoulder

Injuries to young elbows and shoulders are particularly common among gifted athletes in baseball and swimming. These children and their parents represent classic cases of the desire to overdo it with a special talent.

There may be an overwhelming urge on the part of adults, including parents and parent-coaches at children's baseball games, to keep a young pitcher—often as young as nine or ten years old—in a game too long in an effort to win. Or if the child shows great promise as a swimmer, there's a temptation to put in that extra half-hour or hour of practice to gain the edge that may push the youngster up to an Olympic level of performance.

But I can only say, in the strongest possible way, *don't do it!* It's simply not worth it to try to squeeze a little more performance out of a child for a temporary, quite meaningless victory at a very young age. The risk a parent takes for that small triumph may lead directly to serious or permanent injury, and that's hardly a reasonable or intelligent trade-off.

Here's how these injuries may occur. The hardening of the skeleton around the arm and the shoulder hasn't been completed in childhood or adolescence. In particular, there is more cartilage in the elbow and shoulder during the growing, youthful years than in adulthood. When a person is young, the ends of the bones in the joint or connective regions are soft and contain a "growth plate" (the epiphysis) that's the site where further elongation of the bones takes place.

With age, growth stops and the cartilage at the end of the bones "ossifies," or turns into bony tissue. In adulthood, the likelihood of many athletic injuries decreases as a result of the hardening of the bone. But the cartilage and softer bone that are present during the early growth years are more prone to injury because they're not as solid and strong.

So those parts of the youngster's skeleton that are still in the growth stage may be placed at considerable risk during throwing and swimming. The motions may result in overuse injuries to the muscles and tendons of the shoulder because of constant, stressful rotation of the shoulder at the joint. Also, the snapping and follow-through motions during throwing place especially great stresses on the cartilage, nerves, and muscles around the elbow.

How prevalent are these injuries? According to a 1981 report by the U.S. Consumer Products Safety Commission, 20 percent of all baseball pitchers under twelve years of age had pain in their elbows; 48 percent of those aged thirteen to fourteen had such pain; and 58 percent of the pitchers over age fifteen had pain.

The message in these statistics to parents of young pitchers is clear. Monitor their training, and watch and listen closely for any signs of pain or discomfort. The child may not tell you in so many words that his arm hurts because, after all, he probably wants to go on playing. But *you* can often tell by the presence of swelling, difficulty in moving the arm, or wincing when it's touched.

Some of these injuries to the arm have a good outlook for healing and recovery *if* the problem is caught soon enough, *if* the activity is stopped, and *if* the injured part of the body is rested. But in some cases—such as injuries to the side of the elbow—permanent damage may result. Also, the more serious of these injuries may result in arthritis later.

Leg injuries

Overuse of the legs in sports training—especially as a result of distance running or intense training in aerobic sports like soccer—appears to be fostering an increasing number of stress fractures, twisted ankles, sore heels, and strained and pulled muscles and tendons among children.

In general, the best advice for parents seems to be to limit distance running to no more than about one mile, three times a week, for children ten years old and younger. For those over ten up to the early teen years, a two-mile run, three times a week, seems appropriate.[3]

In most cases, injuries from running or other excessive use of the legs may be healed just by rest. Sometimes, though, when the injury is severe, bone fractures or chronic muscle or tendon damage may have to be dealt with surgically.

How can you tell if your child has a relatively serious leg problem? Generally, the symptoms of a stress fracture involve slight pain that increases gradually until the child is disabled to one degree or another. So if you detect pain or soreness that fails to go away after a day or so, or that begins to get worse, see your physician immediately. Loss of use, discoloration, or swelling and pain require attention right away—at least within twenty-four to forty-eight hours. Injuries to leg muscles, tendons, or connective tissues also begin with pain and tenderness in the affected area.

Injuries to the kneecap, which are extremely common among child athletes, have somewhat different symptoms: They are characterized by pain that varies in intensity and may come on either during or after participation in the sport. Knee injuries also may become more painful after the child sits for a long time or tries to climb stairs.

Heat problems

Various treadmill tests have shown that ten-year-old boys have at least the aerobic (endurance) capacity of twenty-five-year-old men. Also, six-year-old girls have capacities that exceed those of twenty-five-year-old women. But this superior aerobic capacity of children shouldn't blind us to the dangers they face from adult training or athletic competition.

As we've already seen, there are special skeletal and muscular concerns a parent should keep in mind in overseeing the athletic endeavors of a child. And there's a second major danger area: heat problems.

Children generate more heat during their sports activities than do adults, but they have less ability to get rid of the heat because they perspire less than grownups. Furthermore, their bodies tend to take in more heat from the surrounding air than do those of older people. All this leads to a high vulnerability to heat exhaustion and heat stroke.

So it's essential to monitor children closely during hot weather and be certain that they're not overcome by the heat. Excessive sweating, flushing of the skin, or complaints of dizziness or nausea may be signs of heat exhaustion. If this happens, the child should stop all physical activity immediately, be moved quickly to a shady, cool spot, and be given plenty of cool liquids.

Even more dangerous, if a child stops sweating and his skin becomes quite hot, he may be suffering from heat stroke. Heat stroke is potentially fatal and requires the immediate attention of a physician. While waiting for the doctor to arrive, parents or other adult supervisors should bathe the child's entire body in cool water or ice, if it's available, to lower the body temperature.

But there's no reason for things to go this far. In the first place, children shouldn't be doing vigorous exercise at all in hot weather, or even in relatively mild temperatures (say, in the seventies) if the humidity is more than about 70 percent.

Also, no matter what the temperature or humidity, children who are exercising and perspiring should be given frequent glasses of water. One suggestion, which seems wise to me, is for children running the equivalent of a two-mile race to drink an eight- to twelve-ounce glass of water thirty minutes before the activity. Then, they should have more water during the activity. This way, they're less likely to become dehydrated and susceptible to problems with heat.[4]

Sports stress.

Children who are pushed too hard, or pushed in the wrong way in sports, may develop certain emotional symptoms and disorders that can seriously damage—and may permanently destroy—their ability to compete successfully and happily.

There are several ways that this "sports stress," as I sometimes call it, can operate.[5] I'd suggest that you use these points as a checklist to evaluate your relationship with your children who are involved in athletics.

1. *Loss of a sense of self-worth or self-confidence.* Children often worry about what their parents, coaches, and teammates think of their performance. If they constantly get negative messages, their sense of self-worth and self-confidence may plummet.

One man, a successful business executive, acknowledged that he suffers now from low self-esteem, and he sees a link between this attitude and his early baseball experience. He said, "My father was my coach. He always pressured me. He yelled at me when I struck out. He expected me to always throw strikes. If the team lost, he would blame me. He never praised me when I did well."[6]

This man was actually a very good pitcher in high school, and he's also a good golfer today. But he worries that he's not as good as other people, and he's still angry with and estranged from his father.

2. *A sour-grape or win-at-any-cost attitude.* Children may also be encouraged to engage in destructive, unsportsmanlike behavior in their effort to win a contest. This aggressiveness may involve engaging in fights, verbal abuse, or intentional fouls.

On a number of occasions, I've witnessed overly enthusiastic eight- and nine-year-old children in a soccer game push one another violently in order to get at the ball. Many times, the coaches ignore the fouls and may even encourage it as a means to intimidate opponents.

The scenes on baseball fields are equally deplorable. Many times, coaches get into shouting confrontations with each other and with umpires. More often than not, the children enjoy the confrontations, participate whenever possible, and come to expect the verbal abuse as a part of the game.

"That's one of the main things I like about playing on these teams!" one nine-year-old told me.

This predilection for violence, excessive aggressiveness, and poor sportsmanship can emerge in numerous unsavory ways. Too often, I've overheard children as young as seven or eight insult and swear at team members from the opposite side when the two groups were passing by each other in the traditional handshaking line after a game.

That kind of behavior fosters mean-spiritedness, sour grapes, and poor sportsmanship that can carry over to later competition, both in the sports arena and outside it. The athletic field used to be a training ground for the building of character. But when adults allow this sort of behavior, without reprimands and proper instruction in generosity and good sportsmanship, the opposite training occurs.

3. *Debilitating anxiety* may also result when a young athlete has too much pressure from parents, from teammates, or from some inner obsession to excel and win.

In general, it's helpful for an athlete to get a little nervous and "on edge" before a match, meet, or game. This "arousal," as it's called, can improve performance.

But when the nervousness escalates out of control, the effect can backfire. The athlete may become immobilized; or in athletic parlance, he may "choke." I heard one tennis player describe this feeling as having a "lead arm" when he prepared to serve. A basketball player may find she can't control the ball or can't come close to the hoop, even with easy shots she usually makes.

Dr. Jon C. Hellstedt notes that if this competitive stress persists over a period of years or seasons, a form of burnout may result—a condition he describes as a "loss of energy and enthusiasm for sports . . . caused by anxiety and stress. The child no longer has fun, becomes overwhelmed by the demands of competition and training, and seeks to escape in order to cope."[7]

Hellstedt believes that this type of stress and burnout may occur as a consequence of excessive adult pressure to win or excel. Specifically, he has found that the problem may arise from adults who consistently give negative evaluations of the child's performance; who are inconsistent in the messages they convey about winning (e.g., they may say "winning isn't everything," but then they get angry when the child loses); or who are overprotective or overly restrictive with the child in sports situations.

When this latter influence is predominant, the child will frequently fail to acquire important coping abilities. Also, he will most likely not develop the independence to operate effectively without the parents' presence.

I'm reminded of one father who was completely committed to having his child become a championship basketball player. But he rarely allowed the boy to play on his own. From the elementary school years, the father always managed to become a coach on the boy's church and intramural teams, and he tried to orchestrate the youngster's every move. The son couldn't dribble, make a pass, or take a shot without Dad's on-the-spot evaluation.

As a result of the father's pressure and hovering presence, the youngster lost any interest in developing independent judgment and creativity in his play. By the time he was in junior high school, he completely lacked any motivation, and he dropped out of the sport altogether in high school.

To prevent these serious sports stress problems, parents and coaches should emphasize the *fun* of sports, especially at an early age. Winning should be an occasion to celebrate—but not to dwell upon.

To be sure, a regular pattern of victories in a sport can be a real confidence-builder. Consequently, I'm a believer in encouraging children to compete only within their age, physical-maturation and skill-level groups so that they can do as well as possible. Getting "wiped off the court" in a tennis match on a regular basis or "smashed" in a soccer or baseball game can be devastating to a child's morale. With too many losses, he may begin to *expect* to lose rather than win, and that expectation can cause him to play at a level well below his potential. Furthermore, a child who competes against those who are bigger, older, or more skilled, will be more prone to injuries.

But still, having said this about the importance of periodic victories, I believe the main parental emphasis and praise should *not* be reserved for a winning season or individual performance. Rather, the parent should focus on how much the individual youngster has progressed and improved in his skills—and how much enjoyment he has received from participation. The *joy* of sports is the key!

Finally, in the effort to avoid too much stress, it's wise to encourage the child to participate in several sports in the early years and to avoid specialization before about age thirteen. Young children simply aren't ready, emotionally or physically, to concentrate on and train in only one sport. Those who are forced to do so will most likely develop the loss of energy and enthusiasm that signals burnout.

If parents develop an intelligent set of responses to challenging athletic conditions, they can help their children avoid most health problems. At the same time, children who are operating within safe boundaries—given their physical limitations, their natural athletic ability, and their age—should be able to enjoy some form of physical exercise to the maximum. These will *not* be kids who have too much sports or fitness training; rather, they will be kids who have just enough—and whose health and self-esteem will benefit significantly from their chosen activity.

▶ *Chapter Ten*

Kids Who Have Too Much—or Too Little—Food

When we think of malnutrition or other food problems occurring in young people, we usually think of poor children in Third World countries or perhaps under-privileged children from poverty pockets in the so-called advanced nations. But major food problems can develop among the affluent—though they arise for reasons other than a lack of money.

Specifically, I've encountered three major challenges to good nutrition among my well-to-do pediatric patients: (1) children who eat too much of the *wrong* kinds of food—including junk foods and foods specifically recommended for adults; (2) those who eat too much of *all* kinds of food and become obese; and (3) children who don't get enough food as a result of eating disorders.

Kids Who Eat Too Much of the Wrong Foods

Many times, as a result of ignorance or neglect, even well-educated and economically well-off parents will fail to give their children guidance in proper nutrition. This problem can begin as early as infancy or in the years before kindergarten.

Anemia is one problem I've encountered among children of parents who are well-intentioned but uninformed—and who certainly have the money to prevent the disease. One mother, a buyer-manager in a local department store, brought her eighteen-month-old girl to see me because the child was looking particularly pale, was exceptionally apathetic, and had been frequently ill with upper respiratory infections.

On physical examination of the little girl, I noticed that she also had a mild heart murmur. So I ordered a blood test and found that her red blood cell count was low. "Your child is anemic," I told the horrified mother.

"How could this possibly happen?" she asked.

To determine the reason, I questioned her further and learned that the child's sitter had apparently been giving the girl excessive amounts of whole milk, usually by bottle when traveling to and from play and at naptimes. When a child drinks too much cow's milk, which contains little iron, the youngster will become filled up on the liquid and may fail to eat other essential foods. Anemia can be the result.

In an individual with anemia, the blood becomes thin and makes a loud noise as it flows through the heart so that a murmur develops. Also, the child may become pale. Though we often think of anemia as a disease of people on the lower rungs of the socioeconomic ladder, well-to-do children may be just as susceptible if there's not someone around to be sure they eat a well-balanced diet.

In this case, the sitter was simply ignorant. She had assumed, "This poor little child misses her mother, so I'll give her a bottle to make her feel better." As a result, the little girl had no appetite left for liver, red meat, iron-fortified cereals, and other foods she needed.

Another problem that may develop with young children is increasing cholesterol deposits as a result of too much junk food and other high-fat foods. But the issue of cholesterol is a complex challenge that must take into account the child's age, physical development, and inherent tendency toward high- or low-cholesterol levels.

A few people—and that includes a few children—don't have to worry so much about eating high-fat, high-cholesterol foods because for them, such a diet doesn't translate into high serum (blood) cholesterol levels. But most children above about age six, like most adults, *do* have to be concerned about fatty foods, which can lead to higher cholesterol levels.

In general, if your child's total cholesterol is above 170 mg/dl (milligram per deciliter) you should take immediate steps to cut down on the youngster's consumption of high-fat, high-cholesterol foods. If his or her total cholesterol reading is above 200, an altered diet and other medical treatment, including cholesterol-lowering drugs, will probably be in order.

There is one major exception to these recommendations about limiting the fats in your child's diet. You'll note that I mention age six as a cut off point for concern about a child's consumption of fats. The reason for this, as I discuss in detail in my previous book *The Brain Food Diet For Children,* is that a child's brain and nerve-sheathing mechanisms are still undergoing significant development in the early years. Proper brain and nerve-sheathing growth depends heavily on the body's use of fats. Probably, this is one of the reasons that God made mother's milk as He did—with a high-fat composition.

Most pediatric and child nutrition experts acknowledge that fats shouldn't be restricted in children under two years of age. Others, like myself, recommend that after the two-year age level, the restrictions should only be eased gradually up to about age six. After passing the six-year age range, a child can and probably should go on a lower-fat regimen, unless there is some other health or nutritional reason to keep fats or cholesterol-laden foods high.

Of course, there are reasons other than cholesterol considerations to avoid junk food. The nutritional level of the high-fat diet typical of a fast-food restaurant is usually much lower than that of a menu consisting of fresh vegetables, broiled fish or chicken, and other such food items. With poor nutrition, bone and muscle development won't proceed at the maximum possible pace. Also, children on a fast-food regimen will often be more obese and have lower energy levels than those who eat more balanced, nutritional meals.

Another rather strange, but still not that uncommon, situation involves affluent parents who have become enamored of so-called health foods. These adults may think they're improving their health and that of their family members by buying most of their food from these shops. And it is quite true that in these places, you can *sometimes* find really healthy and nutritional items that aren't as readily available in regular supermarkets.

But that's not always the case. In a number of instances, I've found that I can buy health food items as cheaply (or more cheaply), and certainly more conveniently, in my regular supermarket.

Furthermore, I urge you if you shop in health food stores to *read the labels!* If you don't, you could end up with a problem that confronted one of my ten-year-old patients.

In this case, the father was the health food enthusiast, and he was also extremely ambitious for his son to become a track star. He found a drink that was advertised as a "high-energy" concoction, and he decided to try out the item himself. Almost immediately, he noticed that his levels of alertness and energy increased after he drank the product. So he bought some for his son and strongly suggested the boy drink two eight-ounce glasses a day.

I got involved when the boy was brought to me because he began to experience problems with his digestion and burning sensations in his chest. I asked the boy if anything was worrying him. He said, "No," and his father told me he was an excellent student with a drive to succeed in school and sports. After doing a thorough exam, I couldn't find anything specific that seemed to be wrong. But while the boy, his father, and I were talking after the exam, I explored the possibility of deficiencies or other problems with his nutrition.

The child's regular diet seemed all right. In fact, the parents fed him more fresh vegetables, fruits, and low-fat foods than most children receive.

Then, the father dropped the bombshell: "Also, he's been drinking a high-energy drink that I started using last fall," he said. "He has about sixteen ounces a day."

"What drink is that?" I asked.

"Actually, I just bought another can before I came here to see you," the man replied, and he pulled a large container out of a sack he had placed on the floor next to his chair.

Upon examining the contents, I immediately identified the problem. The drink contained enough caffeine to keep a bull moose up all night! After pointing this out to the parent—who had failed to check the ingredients on the label—I told him that the boy's problems were probably a combination of a reaction to the caffeine and indigestion.

"Take him off this stuff, and let me know in a couple of weeks how he's feeling," I said.

Sure enough, two weeks later, the burning symptoms were gone, and the child was back to normal.

Caffeine isn't the only danger with such items. The tendency of adults with extra money to buy rich health foods or gourmet foods may also be instrumental in causing another major childhood problem—obesity.

Kids Who Eat Too Much of All Kinds of Food

Some friends of mine had made many trips to Europe, and as part of the image they cultivated, they wanted to eat as much Continental food as possible. Among their preferences were croissants, pâté, "real" butter, gourmet cheeses, and French cuisine, including heavy, rich sauces and high-calorie pastries.

Unfortunately, this fare and a distaste for physical exercise caused significant weight problems in the parents and in their three children. Finally, it became obvious to me that the oldest, a twelve-year-old girl, was having major problems with obesity, and that her two younger brothers were also well on their way toward weight problems. So I frankly discussed the problem with them and their parents.

I said, "You *must* change your diets. These children are going to pay for this 'European' image you're trying to cultivate. They've gotten into terrible nutritional habits, and they'll likely be fighting a weight problem all their lives unless you can turn the situation around very soon."

As it happened, these children were just individual examples of a pervasive American weight problem. Obesity among children aged six to eleven rose by 54 percent between the mid-1960s and 1987, according to a 1987 report in the *American Journal of Diseases of Children*. Furthermore, what the researchers called "superobesity" increased in this age group by 98 percent. As for adolescents—those between ages twelve and seventeen—there was a 39 percent increase in obesity and a 64 percent increase in superobesity.

By the definitions of these researchers, who were from the Harvard School of Public Health, an obese child has body fat that is at or greater than 35 percent over the average of children his or her age. The superobese child has body fat that is at or over 45 percent above the average.

In the case of the family I was dealing with, the main problem was that the parents had established a pattern contributing to the obesity. Also, the entire group tended to be rather sedentary.

"These children should be playing intramural sports," I said. "Doesn't your neighborhood or school have a soccer or basketball league they could join? Or the entire family might take up hiking on weekends. Also, you should walk rather than ride around town. The more you and your children move about, the more calories you'll burn up.

They agreed with my assessment, but changing their lifestyle wasn't easy. In fact, the father, though he meant well, never did become more physically active. The mother, on the other hand, took my nutritional suggestions to heart and began to cook more low-calorie meals. Also, the two young boys got involved in sports, and their extra weight melted right away. The twelve-year-old girl lost some weight, but she continued to have a problem, in part because she had great difficulty launching a more physically active lifestyle.

No one ever said it was easy to lose weight and keep it off. In fact, every dieter I know says it's very, very hard. But if good nutrition and exercise habits are ingrained in a child at an early age, it's likely that those traits will continue into the later years.

In this case, the two young sons have maintained slim, athletic physiques for a number of years, and I expect that they will continue to have only minimal problems with their weight. The daughter, however, is still inclined to be plump. The only thing that seems to keep her from ballooning up to her former level of obesity is the fact that she wants to look as attractive as possible for the boys she is dating.

So we can see varying degrees of success with the weight problems of the children in this family, and the degree of success is directly related to how early good nutritional habits were instilled in the children.

In addition to bad nutritional habits, another factor that may lead to obesity is excessive levels of childhood *stress*. A child may begin to overeat in order to solve some other problem. For example, if a youngster feels unpopular or unaccepted at school, she may turn to food for solace. The food tastes good and gives her a rush of pleasure she's not getting from her peers.

A youngster may put up a wall of fat because of a fear of getting too intimate in relationships. In some cases, a child will have a tremendous fear of failure or inadequacy in dealing with the opposite sex. So to avoid the possibility of rejection or some other threatening encounter, he will overeat. The resulting obesity, he hopes, will cause people to stay away from him.

Others may fear that they'll fail in some athletic challenge. So if they get fat, they'll have an excuse for a losing performance.

Many boys and girls have revealed that they overeat to compensate for a lack of a good relationship with their parents. In other words, a girl may turn in vain to engage in a meaningful conversation with her mother or get her father to pay attention to her. When she fails, she'll turn to food as a second-best outlet for her need for a good parent-child relationship.

This list could continue indefinitely, but the important point is that every parent should regard a child's obesity as a signal. Perhaps the signal just indicates that family nutritional habits are bad. The main problem may be obvious and simple: The parents may be providing the child with too much of the wrong kinds of foods.

On the other hand, the problems may run much deeper. So, with the help of your pediatrician, you should try to sort through the possibilities to find the real source of the weight problem. When you've identified the underlying difficulty, you'll be well on your way to helping your son or daughter overcome the childhood scourge of obesity.

Kids Who Eat Too Little Food

The eating disorders anorexia nervosa and bulimia are insidious nutritional problems among children of all socioeconomic levels. Anorexia involves going on a severely restricted diet, with increasing weight loss. The final result in extreme cases may be death. Bulimia is a disorder that is characterized by eating in binges and then vomiting immediately afterward.

The underlying causes of these problems are complex and not fully understood. But many times, the children are driven by a need to be physically beautiful—even perfect. Also, there is typically a strong need on the child's part to control completely some aspect of her life, namely, her diet.

Usually, these eating disorders afflict young women more than men. I recall one fifteen-year-old girl whose mother was always badgering her about her appearance: "You should let your hair grow longer. . . . You need to exercise your legs more. . . . Those clothes don't suit you at all."

The girl constantly felt she was falling short of her mother's standards of physical looks. No matter how much she exercised or dieted, she never felt she looked quite right. Whenever she would look at herself in the mirror, she would see bulges, skinfolds, or other features that she felt made her unacceptable. So she was constantly on a diet of some sort, and she also jogged and did calisthenics for a couple of hours each day.

Finally, the girl began to get so thin that her mother became worried about her. Then, she fainted while out on an eight-mile run. At that point, the mother made an appointment with me, and during the course of the exam, it became apparent that the girl had an eating disorder, which we finally identified as bulimia.

Typically, bulimia involves normal eating and also binge eating, followed by secret purging of the contents of the stomach. In more serious cases, weight is controlled as well with the use of cathartics and enemas. In this way, the youngster can get some satisfaction from eating favorite, forbidden foods; but then she can avoid the weight gains associated with consuming them. The problem, of course, is that binging and purging undercut a sound nutritional program. Many times, those who regularly vomit after meals end up losing far too much weight and essential nutrients. Consequently, they lack the necessary ingredients to maintain good health.

In this case, the girl was referred to a psychotherapist for counseling, in conjunction with necessary medical treatment. Eventually, she developed a more realistic attitude toward her body and her physical appearance, and she was able to begin to eat normally, without the purging. She continued with her athletics and became an outstanding distance runner. Now, she is happily married, and she believes her husband when he tells her, "I really like the way you look. I wouldn't change you if I could!"

It's ironic that eating disorders like bulimia and anorexia—and also obesity—have been on the increase among the gifted and well-to-do. You might think that children who grow up with all sorts of material and educational advantages would be immune to this sort of problem. But experience shows that the opposite is true.

Having a lot of things and opportunities simply isn't enough to order our lives properly. To maintain good mental and physical health, we need a firm set of values to keep our priorities and those of our children straight. Otherwise, it's likely that weight will careen out of control, health will deteriorate, and the ability to operate as a productive, effective person will cease.

► *Chapter Eleven*

Kids Who Have Too Much Information

Many parents assume that the more a child knows at an early age, the better. But actually, children who are overwhelmed with a flood of facts at too early an age may suffer serious emotional and physical consequences.

In general, many young children tend to talk like a collage of characters from current TV sitcoms and adventure shows. One little girl I saw recently seemed particularly articulate and knowledgeable—until I realized she had strung together a series of stock lines and commercial ad phrases from several popular shows!

Upon close scrutiny, many of these children do *not* have a knowledge of cultural or spiritual facts and concepts that might enrich their lives. They don't know much about classical music, fine literature, or traditional, historic moral teachings. Instead, their little minds have been filled indiscriminately with snippets of pop culture, which have been swallowed without any rhyme, reason, or critical review.

How can this happen? The constant, uncontrolled presence of television is one answer.

If you live in an area where many specialized cable channels are available for viewing, your children are especially vulnerable to informational input that may be too advanced for their age. It's common in many urban areas for the general public to be exposed to frank talk shows, sexually explicit rock music videos, and news programs that present every possible variation of perversion, violence, and other "adult" viewing material. Unfortunately, many parents don't see the TV danger, or they just ignore it because the set makes an efficient baby sitter.

A mother and daughter came to see me because the little girl, who was about eight years old, had been acting unusually rebellious. I noticed immediately that the girl was defiant toward her mother. Also, she tended to use sexually provocative poses, expressions, and profanity that seemed far too advanced for someone her age.

As I explored the youngster's background, I discovered that she spent a great deal of her time during the day with a baby sitter. Also, the child freely admitted that for hours after she came home from school, she watched soap operas with her sitter. She further confirmed something else that I had suspected. The sitter was in the habit of using profane language and was quite free about talking to the child about her own marital and personal problems. The sitter was, in effect, treating the child as another adult.

In short, this girl—through television and exposure to a sitter who indiscriminately shared adult problems with her—found herself in the position of having to handle facts and challenges for which her years had not prepared her. On one level, the girl could talk and act like a little adult. But on a far deeper plane, she couldn't assimilate and deal effectively with all the adult information. As a result, she began to "act up" with her mother in order to relieve some of the tension.

My advice was threefold. I recommended (1) that the mother reduce the amount of time the girl was spending in front of the television set and monitor closely the programs that she did watch; (2) that the parents hire a new sitter; and (3) that they begin to rehabilitate their daughter with more parental attention and influence. This approach was designed to insulate the girl from adult problems and return her emotionally and socially to her own age level.

What Do Pediatricians Say about TV?

Uncontrolled television viewing is the centerpiece of concern about the flow of excessive information to children. Consider these disturbing facts: Children aged two to twelve watch an average of twenty-five hours of TV a week. By the time they graduate from high school, they will have seen eighteen thousand murders and many more robberies, bombings, sexual offenses, and countless other crimes. Furthermore, as I've mentioned in another context, they will have seen about 350,000 commercials.

What do pediatricians say about these developments? They worry first of all that the eleven thousand hours these children spend in their classrooms, and the few minutes a day they spend in "quality time" with their parents, won't offset the messages coming across in the electronic media.

Several other common concerns have been voiced by Dr. Victor C. Strasburger, a member of the Task Force on Children and Television of the American Academy of Pediatrics.[1] Dr. Strasburger cautions parents and physicians about six danger areas, which I've paraphrased below, along with my own observations and comments.

1. *Violence.* More than three thousand studies have linked television violence with aggressive or violent behavior in young people. For example, a 1972 National Institute of Mental Health study stated, "Violence on television leads to aggressive behavior by children and teenagers."

2. *School performance.* Several studies have suggested there is a connection between poor school performance and television viewing. One California report showed that the more television watched by students in the sixth to twelfth grades, the lower scores they got on the California Assessment Program.

3. *Obesity.* I've already discussed this problem in other contexts, but here it is again. Various research into this subject shows that the amount of time a child watches television is a significant predictor of subsequent obesity.

4. *Cultivation of cultural and moral values.* One child development expert, Dr. G. Gerbner, has reported in a 1981 article in *The New England Journal of Medicine* that by the time a child becomes old enough to think for himself, he'll have absorbed more than thirty thousand "electronic stories." These create a "cultural mythology" that determines standards of behavior and belief—and provides a substitute for values that used to be taught by religious institutions. Television sends a child false messages like these:

- Men outnumber women by about three to one, and they lead more interesting lives than women do.
- Elderly people are silly or eccentric.
- Sick, retarded, handicapped, and overweight people play minor roles in life.

▶ The most common—and desirable—occupations are lawyer, doctor, athlete, detective, and entertainer. Jobs that require sacrificial service or large blocks of routine effort either don't exist or don't count for much.

▶ Solutions to life's problems come easily and can generally be wrapped up within twenty-four or forty-eight minutes, or the time it takes to tell a typical TV story.

▶ God, prayer, and religious faith have nothing to do with our lives, except when they provide the framework for some joke.

Clearly, this "world" presented by television has nothing to do with the real world in which you and your children live. But how are these electronic messages being explained or countered in your home?

5. *Sex and drugs.* Television emphasizes that casual male-female relationships frequently develop into sexual relationships. Yet the dangers of pregnancy and sexually transmitted diseases are rarely portrayed. Issues of sexual morality, including the Judeo-Christian prohibitions against premarital and extramarital sex, are almost never presented.

Although the use of narcotics may be presented negatively, alcohol consumption is generally regarded as normal and acceptable in television programs. The health consequences of alcohol abuse, such as alcoholism, deaths resulting from drunk driving, or cirrhosis of the liver, are rarely treated.

6. *Disruptions in family life.* The American family has organized itself according to the day's television schedule. Dr. Strasburger cites these facts from the Nielsen organization: More than 60 percent of American families have altered their sleeping patterns because of TV: (At 9:00 P.M., more than twenty million youngsters aged two to seventeen are watching television, and by 11:00 P.M., 5.3 million are *still* watching!) Another 55 percent have changed their meal times; and a startling 78 percent of families use the television set as an "electronic baby sitter."

Furthermore, many children seem to be more involved with TV than they are with their mothers, fathers, or siblings.

These, then, are the negatives about television that concern many pediatricians. But there are also some positives. Many child development experts give high marks to programs like "Mr. Rogers' Neighborhood," "Sesame Street," "National Geographic" specials, and other educational offerings. In addition, parents can control TV viewing somewhat by participating in the selection of movies and other taped programs that can be watched through the VCR.

I'm reminded of one mother and father who were delighted when their elementary school son became enamored of the movie *Chariots of Fire*. He watched the movie over and over and came to identify closely with Eric Liddell, the Scottish runner who won a gold medal at the 1924 Olympics and then went on to become a Christian missionary to China.

"That movie portrays just the values I want my son to affirm," the father said. "In just a couple of hours, he receives positive messages about sportsmanship, the value of hard work and training, the advantages of athletics, and the priority of Christian values in our lives. Not only that, the movie is interesting and exciting. I couldn't ask for more!"

The key to proper television viewing is parental control. Every parent who wants the cultural flow of information to be a beneficial force in a child's life *must* recognize what a powerful force TV is. If this medium is allowed to intrude freely, with little or no parental guidance in a child's life, the results will almost certainly be destructive. On the other hand, properly used, with regular parental commentary and interpretation, television programs—and related entertainment like videos—may actually support the values that the family wants to promote.

Can Children Read Too Much?

To be sure, many children don't read enough. They spend much of their time watching television and playing, and if they crack a book at all, it's only briefly to do the minimal requirements for a homework assignment.

But there's another concern that has developed about reading. This focuses on the parent who plies her child with so much information from the written word that the youngster becomes overloaded, often with unneeded and perhaps even damaging information. In fact, books for children are the fastest-growing area in publishing, with sales averaging about one-half billion dollars a year. Yet to what extent is this a desirable development, and to what extent is it a negative force?

Here is an overview of some of the questionable childhood reading trends that have emerged in recent years.

Some parents begin reading to their children while they are still in the womb and continue to read two to three books a night in the first year after the child is born. Yet there is no evidence that such a heavy dose of reading, either in the prenatal stage or in the early months of infancy, is helpful. Simple verbal stimulation and play with the child in a nurturing attitude seem to be the most valuable parental endeavors.

Increasing numbers of parents push their children to begin reading before kindergarten, in part in an effort to give their youngsters a head start over their peers. Yet many child development experts feel this kind of pressure may do more harm than good.

Working parents, always looking for time-efficient approaches to child-rearing, have bought more than one hundred thousand copies of Doubleday's *One-Minute Bedtime Stories.* As the title suggests, the parent can whip through one of these stories in only a minute.

Sales of self-help and advice books for children are also on the rise. Some of the topics available: how to improve your self-esteem; how to make friends; how to cope when your parent loses his job; how to deal with divorce; how to prevent sexual abuse. Yet how much of this advice and information is too much for a youngster to handle?

My own feeling is that, overall, the trend toward more reading is a good thing. Clearly, the educational value of reading far exceeds that of television, video games, or similar pastimes.

At the same time, however, it's possible to go too far with certain types of reading. To avoid any excess, I've found a few guidelines to be helpful.

1. Don't force a child to read a second book if she's obviously tired or restless after finishing the first.

2. Don't feel your child must read something every day exclusive of schoolwork. Several times a week is plenty, unless the youngster really wants to read more.

3. If you've set aside a special "reading time" and you encounter resistance, it's not necessary to give up on the reading session altogether. What often works instead is to say, "Well, this is your time to read. But you can choose the book." Or perhaps, "Here are three possible books. Which would you like?" Planning for reading time by having your child select the time is as important as is what to read or how long to read.

4. Selected newspaper or magazine stories can be just as helpful and interesting as a book. I'm reminded of one eight-year-old who had become obsessed with baseball. He watched every game he could on television, collected baseball cards, and incessantly threw tennis balls up against the wall of his room.

Then, in a flash of inspiration, his mother introduced him to the sports section of the local newspaper and helped him find relevant stories on his favorite baseball players. The child immediately became immersed in these accounts and was simultaneously able to satisfy his love of baseball *and* improve his reading skills *and* get used to the idea of perusing a newspaper.

5. Be sensitive to your child's feelings, fears, and interests. If you've experienced a death or divorce in your family, a book on that subject may be appropriate. On the other hand, the child may want to use reading as an *escape* from the worries and cares of the real world. That's a perfectly legitimate purpose for a book or magazine to serve. Trying to force more consideration of a painful subject may exacerbate the child's fears and discourage the view that reading is an enjoyable activity.

An Answer to the Information Explosion: Parental Sensitivity

The main principle I advise parents to observe in overseeing the flow of information to their children is this: *Provide them with facts on a need-to-know basis.*

For example, a five-year-old girl asked her mother a typical where-do-babies-come-from? question. The mother launched into a detailed description of the sex act and human sexuality, and the little girl's eyes glazed over.

The mother, realizing she was doing something wrong, stopped her explanation and went back to the drawing board about how to communicate with her daughter on such an involved topic.

"I knew Allie wanted to know *something* about sex, but I misjudged how much," she finally concluded.

So the next time the subject came up, the mother answered only the question the girl had asked and then fell silent and waited for the girl to respond. This time, the youngster asked a follow-up question: "Where exactly does the baby grow when it's inside you?"

The mother explained and stopped again. That was apparently

all Allie needed to know at that point because she changed the subject and returned to her play.

Gradually, over a period of several years, the full story of sex was conveyed to this little girl. But the information was communicated only in doses that the child could handle.

By the time she was eight or nine, she had the complete biological picture, and she also had been taught certain sexual values and morality. "We believe that sexual relationships are only appropriate between a husband and wife. Sex shouldn't take place outside marriage," the mother had said.

Allie accepted this code of conduct—though at the time she heard it, she couldn't imagine why anyone would want to have sex outside marriage. In fact, she had trouble understanding why anyone would want to have sex at all! In any event, she received and processed only the information that she could handle at the moment, given her age and level of emotional development.

Of course, sex is only one subject that has to be handled sensitively by parents. I've encountered numerous other topics that may trigger such deep-rooted fears in a child that they should be avoided.

One four-and-one-half-year-old boy I know was allowed to watch a graphic television presentation of the possible consequences of a nuclear war. The child became quite concerned about the scenario he was watching. Concern turned to raw fright when his father, hoping to provide an educational end to the evening, went into even more detail about what such a war might involve."

"I realized I had gone way too far when he started crying and then got really angry with me and said, 'Why are you scaring me?' " the father noted.

For months after this incident, the child insisted on including a special provision in his bedtime prayers: "And dear God, please don't let there ever be a nuclear war."

A great deal has been written about a child's fear of war, and there has been some dispute about whether children's fears are real or imaginary. In surveys of children in 1978 and 1983 by Dr. John Mack of the Harvard Medical School, the level of children's concerns about nuclear war was found to be quite high. Other studies have supported these findings, but there has also been criticism of these reports. In particular, some experts say that the concerns being attributed to the children actually reflect fears harbored by parents and researchers.

Whatever conclusions the experts may reach on this subject, one thing is clear to me from my practice. Fear of nuclear war or of various other horrendous events can certainly grip and terrorize a child. Furthermore, it's more likely that child will become afraid if he receives too much information about the topic in question before he's ready for it.

The key, once again, is parental sensitivity. The more knowledgeable a child becomes about the world around him, the better able he should be to cope with challenges. But if the information is excessive or premature, or is presented in a threatening rather than a helpful context, the attempt to educate may fail, and fear may take over. Only the individual parent can discern when full knowledge passes over the line to destructive excess.

Can Information Protect?

We live in an age when there have been many fears that children will be snatched, abused, or otherwise negatively influenced by certain adults. To protect our children, there has been a movement to provide them with information about "how to say no" to strangers, how to identify dangerous adults, and how to otherwise counter threats of abuse.

There's no doubt that a certain amount of information is necessary to prepare children for dangerous situations and to show them how to protect themselves when Mom and Dad aren't around. To this end, many young children these days have been instructed that no one, other than Mommy or Daddy or a doctor approved by the parents, is allowed to touch their "private parts." And they are shown specifically what is meant by "private parts."

Also, children may be taught in various ways not to walk off with a stranger or get into a stranger's car, even if the stranger says he was sent by one of the parents. In many urban areas where drugs and drug dealers are common, children may be taught to stay away from needles, used "crack" bottles, and other such paraphernalia that they may see lying on the street. The same goes for used condoms and other trash that may be particularly hazardous to health.

Obviously, in explaining why the child should stay away from these things, the parent may have to get into an involved discussion about drug addiction, sex, or some other advanced topic. But I think this kind of instruction can be quite helpful and, in fact, is necessary to some degree.

I liken this sort of teaching to what a child living in the jungle must learn about snakes, wild animals, and poisonous plants. No parent in those parts of the world would dream of sending a child out into the woods without some training in the dangers that lurked there. Similarly, we shouldn't hesitate to tell our children what they need to know about the dangers inherent in our streets and society.

But is it possible to go too far with this information? Can we tell our children so much about the dangers that we promote unnecessary fears or worries?

On many occasions, I've encountered children who have been warned to the extreme about the dangers they may face from potential abductors or child abusers. One four-year-old child came to me beset by such serious fears that he couldn't get to sleep at night, and the source of the problem seemed to be information he was getting from his parents. Fortunately, the parents were quite open in talking with me about their approach to protecting the boy.

For example, on one occasion, when the family was going on a vacation, the parents emphasized over and over again that the child should "not talk to anybody" about where they were going.

"We're leaving the house empty and if anybody knows about that, they might come in and rob us," they explained.

But this approach didn't work quite as the parents had planned. When they got into the taxi to go to the airport, the driver asked cordially, "Hello, young man, how are you?"

But the boy, Johnny, just looked at him and didn't say a word.

The driver pressed on: "Oh, it's so nice that you and your family are going to be able to take a trip."

But Johnny just stared and wouldn't say a thing.

Then, the driver asked, "Is this your first airplane trip? Where are you going?"

Finally, Johnny looked at the driver and said, "I'm not supposed to talk to strangers."

"Well, why can't you talk to me?" the driver asked with a twinkle in his eye.

"I'm not supposed to talk to anybody because we don't know who you are and you might rob us"—and with that, the boy withdrew into a silent shell for the remainder of the ride.

In addition to this incident, there were several similar ones that the parents were able to recall in our conversation. Together, they constituted a pattern of worry and fear that had been injected into the child's life in recent months. So I advised the parents to make a conscious effort to avoid references to any warnings or situations that might inspire further fears.

Finally, I proceeded with a routine medical exam and began to pull the boy's pants down, but he started screaming and kicking.

"What's the matter?" I asked the parents.

"Oh, Johnny, it's all right," the mother said, moving over to the boy's side and trying to soothe him. "The doctor can look."

"What do you mean by that?" I asked.

"Well, you know there's so much abuse going on these days that you can never be sure about anybody," the mother replied. "So we've told Johnny that nobody, absolutely *nobody,* is supposed to even get near his private parts besides his father and me."

As I've already said, this sort of parental advice can be healthy and wise—up to a point. But these parents had gone too far, and the child was on the verge of developing a serious set of phobias. It took several counseling visits to help him begin to get rid of some of the most serious parent-induced fears plaguing him.

Another consequence of this overprotectiveness is the problem of what might be called the "sheltered child." Concerned parents these days may tend to get so involved in their child's growth and development that they don't allow him to move toward a healthy independence. In this case, too much information can actually paralyze a child's good judgment and creativity. To put this another way, some youngsters don't develop a kind of "street smarts," which can help in situations where they are required to operate by their own wits rather than by a parent's guidance.

Clearly, there are many dimensions to this issue of excessive information. On the whole, I'm quite positive about many trends that encourage teaching our children more and helping them to become wiser in the ways of the world. But we mustn't move too far or too fast. We mustn't overload them with so much information that they can't process it efficiently. Even more important, we shouldn't introduce them to concepts or facts prematurely when they are at such an immature stage of their emotional or physical development that the information threatens to destroy rather than strengthen.

As we've seen, the Rich Kids Syndrome may be characterized

by a number of attitudes, symptoms, or conditions. Typically, when one or more of the following factors are present, the syndrome is not far behind.

- ▶ To one degree or another, the child becomes an object—a "project" to be developed, a bundle of potential to be realized, a living example of the parents' competence or success or the like.
- ▶ At least 20 percent of the family's net (after-tax) income goes into extras for the child (i.e., expenditures other than those for basic living expenses).
- ▶ The child displays certain telltale emotional or physical symptoms, such as stress-related headaches, stomachaches, or phobias.
- ▶ The child suffers from chronic "overuse" injuries, such as bone pains, muscle tears, or Little League elbow.
- ▶ The child spends large amounts of time away from the parents, usually in the company of parental surrogates, such as baby sitters, nannies, boarding schools, or lengthy camps.
- ▶ The parents frequently push or pressure the child to achieve or succeed in some field.
- ▶ An assumption prevails in the family—or in the thinking of the child—that money or material goods can solve many or most of life's problems and challenges.
- ▶ The parents tend to have rather rigid and demanding notions of child-rearing. ("My child should be reading before kindergarten"; or "My child must be in better physical condition than any of his classmates"; or "My child has to learn at least three new vocabulary words a day.")
- ▶ The child has some nutritional problem or eating disorder.
- ▶ The family lacks a firm set of moral or spiritual values.

Throughout this book, I've tried to suggest ways to overcome this Rich Kids Syndrome. When all is said and done, however, I believe that the most important keys to eliminating this problem are *time* and *values*. That is, the parent should put aside adequate time to interact on an intimate level with the child; and that interaction should occur in the context of a clear-cut set of moral or spiritual standards.

The affirmation of a firm set of family values and the teaching of those values through parental example in practical situations are necessary if your child is to incorporate the most beneficial beliefs and convictions into his or her life. The result will give God, sound morality, and a humane code of conduct a priority over worldly success and achievement.

Furthermore, money and material possessions must occupy a place of importance well below that of good relationships. Selfishness must give way to generosity. The pressure to perform must be supplanted by a dominant impulse to love. The drive toward *having* must make way for the joy of *giving*.

With such an approach, followed daily in family life, parents and children alike can bid good-bye to the Rich Kids Syndrome and to the tragedy of kids who have too much.

Notes

Chapter 2

1. David B. Wilson, "When Children Become an Unessential Item," *Boston Sunday Globe,* September 7, 1986.

Chapter 3

1. Betsy Morris, "Single Parents Who Raise Children Feel Stretched Thin by Home, Job," *Wall Street Journal,* September 28, 1984, 29.

Chapter 4

1. Karen M. Shanahan, et al., "The Children's Depression Rating Scale for Normal and Depressed Outpatients," *Clinical Pediatrics* (May 1987): 245–47.
2. "Symposium: When somatic complaints mask psychosocial disorders," *Contemporary Pediatrics* (January 1985): 20–38.

Chapter 5

1. Deborah Rankin, "The Perils of Raising Rich Kids," *New York Times,* November 16, 1986.
2. Joelle Attinger, "When the Sky's the Limit," *Time,* February 29, 1988, 96.

Chapter 6

1. Ellen Graham, "As Kids Gain Power of Purse, Marketing Takes Aim at Them," *Wall Street Journal,* January 19, 1988, 1.

Chapter 7

1. Ezra Bowen, "Trying to Jump-Start Toddlers," *Time,* April 7, 1986, 66.
2. "What Age for a Child's Music Lesson," *New York Times,* February 19, 1986.
3. Rankin, "The Perils," *New York Times,* November 16, 1986.
4. Gary Putka, "Some Schools Press So Hard Kids Become Stressed and Fearful," *Wall Street Journal,* July 6, 1988, 1.
5. William J. Warren, "Tutoring Becomes a Tool to Provide an Edge," *New York Times,* July 20, 1988, B–7.
6. Jan Herman, "Lost Childhood," *New York Daily News,* Extra–II.
7. Ibid.

8. Barbara Starfield, et al., "Morbidity in Childhood—a Longitudinal View," *New England Journal* 1984, Vol. 310, 824–829.

9. W. Thomas Boyce, "Stress and child health: an overview," *Pediatric Annals* (August 1985): 539, 541.

10. Ann S. Masten, "Stress, coping and children's health," *Pediatric Annals* (August 1985): 543, 546.

11. Mary Ann Lewis and Charles E. Lewis, "Psychological distress and children's use of health services," *Pediatric Annals* (August 1985): 555, 558.

12. Ibid.

Chapter 9

1. Marilyn Wellemeyer, "Fitness for Your Kid," *Fortune*, October 27, 1986, 140.

2. Mark I. Pitman, "Sports injuries in children," *Resident and Staff Physician* (September 1986): 47ff.

3. Thomas W. Rowland and Peter P. Hoontis, "Organizing road races for children: special concerns," *The Physician and Sportsmedicine* (March 1985): 126–32.

4. Ibid.

5. See Jon C. Hellstedt, "Kids, parents, and sports: some questions and answers," *The Physician and Sportsmedicine* (April 1988): 59–71.

6. Ibid., p. 60.

7. Ibid., p. 68.

Chapter 11

1. Victor C. Strasburger, "When parents ask about the influence of TV on their kids," *Contemporary Pediatrics* (May 1985): 18–30.